BUDGET SPAGHETTI

The Cozy Way to Craft a Budget That Feels Like Home

By Anne Serrano, CFP®

With a Foreword by Gloria S. Garcia Cisneros, CFP®
and artwork by Masami Kiyono

Published by:
Executive Books | Tremendous Life Books
P.O. Box 267, Boiling Springs, PA 17007
717-701-8159 | 800-233-2665
www.TremendousLeadership.com

Paperback ISBN: 978-1-961202-90-0
Ebook ISBN: 978-1-961202-91-7

Grandma,

Thank you for the only constant cozy home and kitchen throughout my childhood and young adulthood. You never thought you were good at numbers or finances or tech, but when it came down to it, you were able to learn and take care of so much more than you'd ever imagined you could. I wish there had been someone earlier in your life to talk with about these things, so that you wouldn't have to learn it all while Grandpa's dementia was progressing. I love and miss you both every day.

You did so much for everyone. This one is for you.

CONTENTS

FOREWORD

Long before I became a financial advisor, I learned some of my most important money lessons in my grandmother's kitchen. I just didn't know they were money lessons at the time.

When I was growing up, my grandma made spaghetti. Her recipe was a can of tomato puree, noodles, and ground beef. Super simple. To this day, it's still my favorite spaghetti. As a kid, I never questioned the ingredients. It tasted like home. It tasted like being cared for.

Recently, as an adult, I was cooking with my grandma when I mentioned that I still made spaghetti exactly the way she made it for me growing up.

She chuckled and told me something I had never considered. If she could have afforded it back then, she would have bought the prepared sauce, the Ragú with the seasonings already mixed in and the fancy meatballs. The shortcuts that made life easier. But money was tight, and like so many lower income families, she stretched every dollar she had to make sure there was food on the table.

What I remembered as a cherished family recipe was also a financial decision.

Funny how that happens. Our earliest money lessons aren't taught through formal conversations or in a classroom. They're learned through observation. We watch the people we love make choices, sacrifices, and tradeoffs. We inherit their habits, their worries, their resourcefulness, and sometimes even their fears.

We inherit recipes. And often, we don't realize where those recipes came from until much later.

That's one of the reasons I immediately connected with Anne's *Budget Spaghetti*.

This isn't a book about achieving financial perfection. It's not about having the perfect spreadsheet, savings rate, or plan. Instead, it is an invitation to approach money with curiosity instead of judgment. To notice what's already in your pantry before rushing out to buy new ingredients.

Trust me, doing what I do for a living I know how intimidating financial conversations can be. Many people believe they need to be a completely different person before they can get their finances "right." They assume they need more wealth, more discipline, more knowledge, or more willpower before they're "allowed" to begin.

Anne offers something refreshingly different. She starts with compassion.

Throughout these pages, you'll find gentle guidance, thoughtful reflection, and practical encouragement. Rather than focusing on what you've done wrong, I hope you notice what's already working. Rather than asking you to overhaul your entire life, Anne invites you to take one cozy step forward.

Because financial confidence rarely appears overnight. It's built in small moments. It's built when we give ourselves permission to learn. It's built when we stop measuring ourselves against others' recipes.

We all begin from different places, with different ingredients and recipes handed down through generations.

The goal isn't to judge those recipes. The goal is to understand them. To appreciate what got us here and work with what we got.

And then, with intention and care, decide what we want to keep, what we want to change, and what new traditions we want to create.

In many ways, this book feels like a conversation between generations, honoring the resourcefulness that got us here while helping us build the confidence to go somewhere new. I found myself thinking about my own grandmother, whose version of spaghetti taught me lessons about resilience long before I understood anything about budgeting. Perhaps you'll find yourself thinking about someone who shaped your own relationship with money or possibility.

Because money is rarely just about money or numbers. It's about the stories we inherit, the values we carry forward, and the future we're trying to build.

Wherever you are in your relationship with money, I hope you'll approach these pages with an open mind and a little self-compassion. Give yourself some grace!

From one friendly Certified Financial Planner to the younger version of herself who didn't grow up knowing much about the world of personal finance, let me stress this:

You don't need to have everything figured out, because none of us ever fully do. You just need a willingness to begin.

Like any good meal, confidence is built one ingredient at a time.

Gloria S. Garcia Cisneros, CFP®
June 2026

INTRODUCTION

Cozy, Really?

What is the first thing you think of when you hear the word budgeting?

And the next thing you think of?

How far down the list would you have to go to get to "cozy"?

Probably pretty far down the list! Or if you're like most people, "cozy" would not come up at all.

More likely, you thought of numbers. Perhaps at a store checkout or in spreadsheets or apps with indecipherable columns. Depending on your experience, you may also have thought of being told to skip the latte or the streaming service. Perhaps it feels like a messy closet you would never show anyone, and you don't even want to go in there yourself. Maybe you do have some understanding of where your cash goes, but it doesn't feel possible to ever think of it as "cozy."

You may, in fact, have an immediate negative reaction to the idea of a cozy, comfortable budget. A comfortable budget may seem the opposite of what you have come to understand a budget to be.

Many people learn about budgeting as a set of restrictions. In this way of thinking, a budget is a set of paternalistic rules to prevent us from buying the things we want to buy. The only allowable free rein is to judge ourselves or others for buying things that we can't justify as absolutely necessary.

If this is your experience with budgets, the concept of coziness may seem hopelessly out of place—a sign of reckless optimism at best or toxic positivity at worst. You likely recognize the intense difficulty (sometimes near-impossibility) of balancing the cozy and the realistic. You may have concerns that anything in a budgeting book about coziness will be too easy or basic to be useful in any practical circumstances.

In honor of this practicality, let's consider a definition.

In its purest form, a budget is a plan or intention for your money. Typically, this is the money that you receive or use on a daily basis (also known as your cash flow).

There are many different ways to budget: an awareness of the cash flowing in and out, detailed accounting for every single cent, looking at your monthly spending reports from your various bank or credit accounts, and more.

Through paying some attention and setting your intention, a budget brings a general sense of where the money's going. Without attention and intention, a budget document is merely a sketch of what an organized closet could look like. It won't be yours until you make it so.

But let's come out of the closet and into the kitchen. In this book, you will learn how to craft a budget that works for you and how to fine-tune your existing strengths and systems. Yes, you already have strengths and systems.

If you have a purpose for the money you use, you are already budgeting. And then it just becomes a question of "Are you budgeting in a way that is helpful for what you want and need in life?"

Like money, a budget is a tool to support and facilitate having the resources needed for life. The purpose of a kitchen is to cook up your necessary nutrients, not to have a picture-perfect cabinet and countertop combo.

A cookbook is not about building cabinets, and this book is about your practice of budgeting, not the vast array of strategies, cabinets, and appliances available to organize or prepare your money. There are lots of apps, programs, and methods for tracking cash flow. The options available will always change. And you will always be the one to use them for your purposes.

Budget Spaghetti is not in itself a budgeting method, but rather a process to discover, experiment, and enjoy your own. Through this twelve-week process, you will craft a method of budgeting that works for you, balancing your needs for awareness, coziness, comfort, and momentum towards your goals. Each chapter is designed to be taken one week at a time.

This steady, methodical pacing honors the layers of work involved in showing up to a habit-creating book like this. And as you work on each week's activities and reflections, know that you may move comfortably through each chapter at your own pace. Even when life happens and a week becomes too full of other obligations, you can choose to stay with a chapter for a little bit longer.

Over the course of these chapters, week by week and day by day, you will not only be developing a budget practice but making the gradual changes for a shift in mindset. On the foundational level, you will be moving from a fixed mindset about budgeting (most commonly "I'm just not good at numbers") to a growth mindset, journeying from avoidance of rote memorization to the joy of active discovery. If your budget is a love language, the ultimate expression of self-care is not mere literacy but cozy lifelong learning. And as you build that foundation, you will move from negativity to nourishment, and from sustenance to comfort.

Each new stage or season may have different needs, but what you are practicing here is how to learn and grow and find support. These practices will help not just in the circumstances of one season but also in unexpected or changing days or seasons. Putting this into practice is therefore not something that can be done all at once. It will involve layering in lessons and learning over time, always coming back to the meals and momentum that nourish and sustain.

One of my needs in life is the cozy feeling of home. Even if I'm not at home, I thrive when I can have at least a little of the space, mindset, or routines that bring me comfort. Budgeting did not start out cozy for me. My dad started me budgeting my dollar-a-week allowance when I was in second grade. For over a decade, I thought it was a punishment for taking money from the piggy bank for the book fair. Ever since then, I have had many different ways to budget and convince myself to budget. I have rebelled against budgets set for me, and I have avoided my own budgets.

Still, I have seen the power of budgeting. While I could fall back on the habit of budgeting, I didn't have the challenges of learning to manage money with tough things going on. I remain impressed by college classmates who were first learning personal finance during a financial crisis. In my early work, my roommates, early colleagues, and I were just scraping by while working to exhaustion. I have seen countless examples from my volunteering and budget coaching to the case studies in my Master's degree in Financial Planning. And during my journey to becoming a CFP professional, I had the heart-wrenching privilege of being present with my grandparents, especially my grandma as she learned to budget while my grandpa was declining with dementia.

We all have the need and capacity to get through so much, just by virtue of living in this world—but if you are in a place of relative safety, why not get a little head start on budgeting? Like prepping a crockpot meal before a strenuous workweek, doing some budget prep can ease the burden on your future self. Practice it a little bit and let it become muscle memory. Even if you don't use it with intention unceasingly (and really, that sounds exhausting, so maybe don't do that), practicing now will give you support in those future moments when you can make use of it.

Whether you're in an easy moment or somewhat tougher moment of life, this book will have useful practices. (If you're in a financially difficult moment, check out the Safety Disclaimer and resources first. After you take that step, give yourself a mental high five. This book will be here when you get back to it.)

Traveling into the unknown can be scary, and even a smooth journey toward doing something important and meaningful can raise fears and doubts. Look, I'm an introverted homebody who would almost always much rather be hanging out with my cat than talking in a room full of people, but sometimes I meet the best and nerdiest random people that way. The comfort and coziness of intentional budgeting are in moments from the mundane to the extraordinary, in the joyful celebrations or quiet evenings, the inspiring vacations or cups of tea while watching the rain.

This book is the starting point, not the answer to everything. Sometimes you need to ask someone who actually cooks that recipe more often. Sometimes the trendy methods won't work in certain situations like yours.

Sometimes your kitchen layout, appliances, or supplies don't match up perfectly with the recipe.

There are so many times when we want there to be just one answer. But really, would you want to only have one possible meal? No. There are different circumstances, different experiences, different stages in life, different needs, and we are all in different places as we come to read this (or any) book.

Whether you are just starting out on your financial journey, turning the page for a new chapter, looking to a next step or goal in your financial life, the specific strategies will be different. Starting to build an emergency savings will involve different tactics than getting ready to make a career or housing decision.

This is foundational stuff: becoming more willing and practiced at looking, being honest about what you want now, what you find yourself wanting or needing more or less of, and what you anticipate of your needs for the coming days, weeks, months, or even years. It can be nerve-wracking because of past experiences or simply because of the insurmountable truth that the future cannot and will not ever truly be known.

Even so, you will find that thinking about money can be a safe, comfortable, and even cozy experience. Like anything cozy or worthwhile, it takes some ingredients, time, energy, and practice.

In each chapter, you will find a short reading that you can return to throughout the week. The reading will describe the key content and strategy, while sharing some budgeting stories related to the topic.

Each week's reading wraps up with an Action Step for you to take, followed by the Cooking Journal prompts for the week.

The first part of each week's Cooking Journal will be jotting down your Top 3 Priorities for the week. Whether budget, work, personal, or anything in between, these priorities are the things to complete for this week to be a success. If a priority feels too big to start, take a few extra moments to ponder what is actually involved in completing the task. Very often in this process, people find that what they'd thought was "just one easy task that I should've been able to complete by now!" is actually at least a dozen subtasks. The good news is that at least one of those subtasks (if you've broken them down into small enough bites) will be able to get done much easier now that you can see it.

Your Cooking Journal can be a physical or digital notebook and can include multiple mediums depending on what suits you (perhaps sticky notes, a spreadsheet, a canvas, a sketch journal, or something else). Different things may work at different times.

As you explore, learn, noodle it over, and experiment in the Budget Kitchen, your Cooking Journal will be the space for you to take notes on your findings and priorities, reflect on concepts from the week's readings, and solicit assistance from your sous chef, your Successful Self from the future.

Yes, this is also a nerdy time travel book, and your mind is the time machine. Let's go.

Introduction: Action Step

Write a note to your future self at the end of this book. Make it kind and conversational, including the answers to these questions:

1. What is your hope or goal for your future self at the end of this book?
2. What are your top 3 priorities for these 12 weeks?
3. What do you hope you will be able to accomplish in 10 years, 20 years, or next year?

Disclaimer

Safety first!

While every effort is made for this book to be accessible for everyone, there is an essential truth to acknowledge.

This book is designed to be used by people who are already in a place of relative monetary safety. The steps and timeline described here are not to be used if a person is, for example, in immediate danger of the kitchen burning down.

There are outside services for circumstances of extreme financial hazard and danger, just as there are emergency services for dangerous situations in a regular kitchen. It would be irresponsible for me not to mention that if the kitchen is burning down, you should call the fire department. In cases of financial danger, it can be difficult to know who to call, so there are a few resources at the website on the last page of the book.

A note about the resources provided: There are plenty of possible hazardous financial circumstances that require different services to assist. Because too many choices can be overwhelming, the list is not exhaustive. For those of us who grew up before cell phones, we likely had a couple of phone numbers stuck to the side of the fridge, the first call in case of emergency. Consider the resources at the back of this book a lifeline. If the resources listed are not the exact resource you need in this moment, chances are that these brave, kind-hearted people will be able to point you in a helpful, healthy direction.

If you are in some financial danger—whether from the crushing weight of debt, having your financial autonomy restricted by a controlling substance or partner, a loss of income or shelter, pressure to pursue a financial product which you are not sure about, among so many other possibilities—please reach out to one of the included resources for assistance.

If you have been in or are currently in one of these places, you know this is such a difficult place to be, and it can be hard to even look around. You are not alone.

It can take some time and effort to get out of financial danger. Know that these emergency fridge resources are here to guide you now, and that once you are in a safer place, this book is here for you to return to as well.

Part I

OBSERVE

Wherever you are in this moment, pause. Breathe in deeply, hold for a moment, and slowly exhale the entire breath. Then, if you wish, exhale a little more. Breathe in and notice something good. This may be something in your environment or simply that you are taking a moment to breathe right now. Let that breath go.

Keep breathing.

This process of budgeting is about creating something as versatile as spaghetti. A simple spaghetti meal is a relatively easy dish to prepare. As long as you have the right kind of noodles and sauce, you can generally appease a good deal of picky audiences, whether kids, neighbors, in-laws, or yourself. While a budget spaghetti can be a way to put together nourishment swiftly, it can also become more nuanced and flavorful as you develop your own style and taste.

We learn in the kitchen by repetition, by doing things over and over in varying conditions and with different moods or seasons. Similarly, we will learn in our budget kitchen to return with compassion and grace to practice and grow.

The purpose in this first stage is to get more comfortable thinking about the concept of money and budgeting. No need to make any changes or plans quite yet. You will begin to notice without judgment when there are thoughts, circumstances, or moments that are relevant to this journey. Without judgment means that whether things seem positive, negative, important, unimportant, or neutral, you can notice what you think and feel.

You will also notice that you don't need to make more of these judgments. Just notice and be.

This month, there will be times when you are feeling calm and safe, and times when you experience discomfort or uncertainty. In all of these, practice being safe in that moment—and it does take practice! As with any craft, an instance that doesn't feel successful is still an essential part of learning.

Through it all, you are practicing gratitude for your attentiveness to yourself. You are finding kindness and compassion, understanding what you can change and what is beyond your control, and most importantly, simply being present in that moment. You are present even (or perhaps especially) when sometimes it means turning off the stove and going to another little space to just breathe for a few seconds.

This book is designed to be used regularly and gradually layered in over time. As you go through this process, expect to find a lot of things that you would prefer not to look at too carefully. This may feel more or less true for you at various stages of this journey, so remember this: You don't have to look at it all at once. This part of the journey is not about looking at everything fearlessly or appearing to crush it, but about showing up for few more seconds each day, practicing through a variety of days and circumstances, and moving from moments of avoidance to more presence and awareness.

WEEK 1

Welcome to Your Budget Kitchen

Think about a time you have felt cozy.

Perhaps it is around a campfire or watching a sunrise. Perhaps it is in a community group where everyone has gathered for a potluck meal, and you only had to prepare one side or entrée and you arrive and you can already smell all the incredible dishes, prepared with love and kindness by neighbors, friends, family. Perhaps it is curled under a blanket with some hot cocoa and a book, with nobody else around.

All of these experiences of coziness really do exist, and hopefully you have had some such experiences yourself.

Each cozy moment takes preparation to set up, and some knowledge as well.

For watching a sunrise, it involves knowing when the sun will rise. Perhaps it involves setting an alarm or getting to bed at a time when you'll have enough sleep or taking a moment in your workday or commute to glance or watch.

Preparing an item for a potluck involves knowing a community where you want to gather together, perhaps hearing what sort of foods they might need for this meal, or simply knowing your favorite food (spaghetti or otherwise) to prepare or bring to a potluck. Either way, it involves knowing a bit about the options, choosing one or the other, and then doing all the steps in our busy days to make the food (and ourselves) show up at the time when we are planning to do so.

To be curled under a blanket with hot cocoa and a book with nobody else around, you need to set aside that time. That can be a difficult choice on days when time and tasks just get away from you, and nearly impossible in some stages of life and some households. And if you succeed at that most difficult of quests, you still also need to prepare the hot cocoa, perhaps even replenish your hot cocoa supply ahead of time, and select the book you want to read, setting aside any devices and worries for the day to fully be in that moment. No small feat in this digital world!

Even cozy things take some preparation and setup to make it happen. That does not negate the coziness we feel when we are in the moment. It is just a part of the process and practice of coziness.

Where then do we start for our cozy budget? The same place we start with any of these cozy moments. We start with arriving.

As in the example of the seemingly simplest cozy task of hot cocoa, arriving sounds easy, but it can be the most challenging part in the chaos or busyness of life. For that reason, we will take our time and practice gratitude for any time when we are able to arrive.

With every client I have seen, and every person I have spoken with, showing up is the first win. It is the hardest win, and it is accomplished when thinking intentionally about money, no matter what that might look like for you at first. In the beginning, it simply means acknowledging interest or a desire for something to end up being useful. Recognize that the acknowledgment itself is a win.

Your Budget Kitchen

To start, let's create a cozy, safe place to think about our money: what we have, how we spend it, what we want to create with it. Let's imagine a "budget kitchen," a cozy comfortable safe place to breathe, to explore new ways of creating new things, to boldly meet with a compassionate friend (or future version of yourself) who knows you are capable.

I imagine a place where I can pause, breathe, and have a nice calming sip of tea. I love looking at trees and their leaves, so no matter the time of year, I frequently imagine the foliage outside is lush and comforting. Even without leaves, the nourishment flows up from the roots.

The branches are adorned with the morning dewdrops, each droplet a world in miniature, reflecting the life around it, glistening in the light. In my mind, my budget kitchen has a window to this calming scene, and a chair beside that window where I can sit and breathe at any time, reveling in the calming beauty of life proceeding without any of my own input or output.

The feeling of a warm cup of tea, cradled in my hands or perhaps held to my heart as I listen to the birdsong. In this mental landscape, I am still recharging, even as I turn my mind from the window and towards the essentials of living, of breathing, of the alchemical process of combining the elements of nourishment into a meal that will support my sustenance and fuel my goals.

My budget kitchen is a place in my mind where I have decided it is safe to exist, to practice, to show up, to breathe. I can organize it as I wish, and every resource available to me can be where I want, need, or expect it to be. Even when the mental landscape is cluttered, I can anchor in the pockets of calm, and I find that it is safe and good to breathe here, to be here.

The budget kitchen is a mental landscape unique to each person. It is the place where we encounter money and make use of it. In building and maintaining a healthy, cozy budget kitchen, this is a place where you feel like you can breathe, practice, not-know, experiment, learn, create. It is where you will meet with your brave, compassionate, determined self, the one who knows that you are capable and still meets you where you are.

You are here to make what nourishes you and then grow from there.

Who's there?

When we begin to explore budgeting, we find that far from generating an empty mental space from scratch, there are not only existing kitchen elements in there, but sometimes also people and memories.

We often find ourselves in our budget kitchen with our past selves and past or present friends, family, acquaintances, and even people from media or popular culture. It can get a bit crowded in there, but nobody needs to be in there but you. You're not kicking these mental avatars out for good, but just saying, "I'll see you another time. For now, I need some space for myself."

As the guests (wanted or unwanted) begin to depart, you may begin to notice another presence: your potential future selves.

Many of these possible future selves contain ingredients you recognize from someone you have probably thought of a lot, and who you will contemplate a bit more this week: your Successful Self. In the Cooking Journal, you will imagine a Successful Self from one of your possible futures. Who is this person? What does your Successful Self hope for, enjoy, and value? Where do you live? How do you spend your time? What do you do with extra money? What do you save for? What do you give?

Your Successful Self is here because they know that this is part of their origin story, part of how they made it through to all the cozy comfort they now have. And just like when you think it of your past selves, your Successful Self looks at you and thinks, "Wow, I've learned a lot since then, but I couldn't have gotten to where I'm at without getting through all that. Thank goodness, and thank you, Self."

With the gratitude expressed, imagine that even as you continue to feel their gratitude, your awareness of their presence fades, and you are now alone in your peaceful, cozy budget kitchen, ready for the next step in the journey.

Kitchen Safety

Have you ever watched (whether in person, in a cartoon or movie, or a scene in a book) a young person walk-run-flail-dance through a kitchen, blissfully oblivious to the corners, sharp edges, or heat elements and their possible effects?

None of us start off knowing how to safely be in any given space, but whether by discussion or disaster, we learn some safety basics. If we were not too precocious, some of those lessons were introduced before we got any scars, most likely as ground rules.

Ground rules help keep a kitchen safe. You know the ones. Don't run with scissors, walk if the stove is on or someone's slicing veggies, no roughhousing in the kitchen, and the timeless classic: don't touch the stove when it's on or hot.

As in any cozy, safe kitchen, let's start with some ground rules.

Ground rules enable your use of the mental and emotional landscape of your budget kitchen to cultivate a safe place to learn and grow.

When mistakes happen, notice the chance to grow. Where the grime of shame or guilt appears, recognize it with nonjudgmental compassion. Just like the sauce splatter while cooking, it doesn't need to stay on the counter. This time around, perhaps a little messiness was a part of getting essential nourishment. Next time may be more or less messy, but you will still need nourishment every day.

In your budget kitchen, the ground rules can really be summed up as: Be nice (actually nice) to yourself; don't be a bully; and don't diminish your own self and efforts. To sum it up quicker: What you do matters. Do it with self-kindness.

You will find that the budget kitchen is often messy and imperfect—and still nourishing. Comfort and coziness are attained through purposeful momentum. This is not a stagnant space, especially not when resting. True rest is essential, and there are enough barriers to attaining it without piling on shame. If you can disconnect from the never-ending to-dos, notifications, and binge-watching, you will find nourishment in even a few seconds of purposeful rest.

These ground rules are essential when developing a place to learn and grow, because we all come back to our budget kitchens whether we notice it or not. (Even in the times when we choose to avoid it, the budget kitchen is involved in the decision.) Since we have to come back around it, it would be nice to enjoy it as well, so that we want to come back.

Remember that true kindness is not the same as being polite or complacent. As with a teetering toddler wobbling into the kitchen, kindness involves safety, learning, and growth. Similarly, while addressing uncomfortable money matters, rather than sprinting through the kitchen or just not even going in, it is a kindness to pause, let yourself truly arrive, and then take the steps you need to in a safe and timely manner.

Remember, you can't ever make all the progress at once, because you can't actually be in more than one time at once. Progress comes from coming back, especially in the face of the unexpected. And that's just the thing, because to come back, you have to arrive each time.

For the duration of this budget journey, you will really just need two essential tools: moments of practice and a cooking journal to record that practice. Keep jotting down these notes on a regular basis. This "cooking journal" will require finding those little moments when you can breathe, observe, and eventually reflect.

Whether it is a reflection on the questions or a satisfying checkmark next to the date: Hurray! You showed up. Savor that moment of noticing that you are building this safe, cozy kitchen habit.

Remember: if you can't feel safe to explore and try something new, you will end up staying where you are.

For many of us in our budget kitchens, safety is progress.

Kitchen Ground Rules

1. Breathe. You can feel safe and energized here.
2. Be kind to yourself here: Appreciate any good effort.
3. Use this space safely, for yourself and others.
4. Take a deep breath and deal with one thing.
5. Remember that you can turn off the stove.
6. Don't try to rebuild the whole kitchen while the stove is on.
7. Design a space and mindset that you want to come back to.
8. There are multiple ways to do things well: find a cozy step forward.
9. Progress is a result of coming back.
10. Coming back is the win.

Action Step

Write yourself a message from your Successful Self Place it somewhere you will see it this week.

Remember: Your Successful Self is grateful for each step you're taking in your Budget Spaghetti journey, because your Successful Self can see how every small win (and every stumble) has accumulated and evolved over time into their cozy, comfortable budgeting that feels like home.

Cooking Journal

Top 3 Priorities for the week ahead

1. What are your Top 3 Priorities this week? Write them down.
2. If a priority feels too big, break it into sub-tasks until one is completely doable today.
3. When there are a lot of tasks on the list, which are the three most important? What step can you take today? What must be done by next week?

Reflection Questions

1. The Journey Here
   When you think about money or finances, what thoughts or emotions come up? What experiences are you growing from as you begin this journey? Have you tried budgeting before? What happened when you did well? How were some ways you have successfully avoided tripping hazards in the past?
2. Arriving in the Budget Kitchen:
   What does your Budget Kitchen look and feel like? Where will you sit and breathe? How do you feel when you think of arriving now? What do you hope for in 12 weeks?
3. Awareness of the Budget Kitchen:
   Notice when you use money or think of current or past goals. Don't shut out any thoughts or emotions. Be sure that as you observe you also follow the Ground Rules.

What Would My Successful Self Do? (WWMSSD?)

1. Meet My Successful Self exercise*
   i. Describe your Successful Self's life. Where do you live? How do you spend your time? What does your Successful Self's relationship with money feel like?
   ii. What does your Successful Self do with surplus money? What do they save for? What do they give?
   iii. What would your Successful Self tell you, right now, about where to begin?

* Note: As you write, do not consider what is possible. If something seems impossible, write it down anyway.

Week 2

Survey the Pantry

Imagine you're cooking for the very first time. You can't assume you'll make a world-renowned spaghetti (or other meal). If you're like me, you're just hoping not to make a mess while making a somewhat edible meal.

Even following a recipe exactly (assuming you found a tasty one!), depending on that day's environment, tastes, or mood, the meal might not taste quite the same each time. And when it tastes good, it may not look as appetizing as you feel it should. Sometimes you try to make it look right; other times you eat that tasty-enough spaghetti mess and call it a day.

Every day, we use our available resources: time, money, attention, energy, skills, experience. We want to manage our money well, and logically, we can't expect to know right away what will work for us. Still, we search all the "simple hacks" for managing money, and we imagine there are people following all the rules we've ever heard of for a perfectly healthy budget and compare ourselves against this impossible standard as if it were a basic starting point. Sometimes we expect this of ourselves. Sometimes we perceive (or are told from bold headlines) that it is expected of us.

And so, our previous, default budget kitchen may have been a place where we were a bit too practiced at feeling the shame or burden for not knowing, not being "self-made," not doing all the things "right" just like everyone else did "back in the day." That picture-perfect nostalgic myth is always going to be impossible to live in real life.

It doesn't make sense to assume you can just walk into the budget kitchen for the first time and know exactly how to make a healthy, nourishing masterpiece right away. It is daunting to begin a new craft. There is so much to know, and it's hard to know where to begin. For this week, all we actually need to know is how to look in the pantry.

Awareness is one of the most important, most challenging, and most skipped steps in budgeting. Often, people expect to immediately begin to change how and what they are "supposed to" spend on. The first behavior change is more subtle, but even more important: changing how (or even whether) one notices. Like breath, notice what goes in and what goes out. Notice how the experience feels. Remember: no judgment, just awareness.

These first weeks, no matter how great the temptation to go big, the most essential actions to take are arriving and observing. Put those together over time, and you will find you've cooked up some quality awareness sauce. Intentional behavior change begins with awareness, and the changes stick through practice and experimentation later on.

The Budget Kitchen Pantry

Whenever I'm in a different kitchen, I can't find anything. Even in my own kitchen, things might not have the logical flow for my brain in that moment. I could forget where something goes, or the kids may have put the scissors with the forks (hey, you know it's a win that they're in any drawer).

The good news: you get to rearrange your budget kitchen just by thinking about it, and you don't have to keep it all organized in your head. Whenever you jot down a thought or realization in your Cooking Journal, you are gathering and processing important data. Over time, you will begin to notice the topics, patterns, and possibilities in what you are observing.

Like a quick spaghetti after a long workday, with people or pets clambering for our attention and care, the primary goal of our first quick budget spaghetti is simply to have the nutrients needed to live.

Or to be more concise, the goal is living.

Assuming you're not a ghost, zombie, or vampire, put a checkmark right there: Living? Check!

You are already using a budget kitchen every day. You are taking care of your needs enough to keep living to make it to (and through) this day.

To be able to keep living, you need relatively good food. Yes, "relatively," as in better than the alternative.

Listen, there have been (ok, sometimes still are) times when I ate a lot of fast food. It was easy, and it took less energy staying seated during a long commute than preparing anything at home. Meanwhile, there was a trade-off not just in the monetary cost, but also in the quality of ingredients. It worked well enough for me at the time, and eventually I did get a job with less of a commute and gradually layered in a few simple home-cooked meals to enhance my nourishment.

To keep attaining that goal of living, you need relatively good nutrients that take the right amount of energy and effort to prepare in this season of your life and in a recipe that is enjoyable enough that you actually choose to use them.

Beyond money or physical goods, you also have experience and skills used in other circumstances. It's like looking at a can of beans, knowing what you usually make with it, and thinking of other possible recipes you have heard of, experienced, or even made yourself. These skills are some of your available resources, and you use your budget kitchen skills more often than you think.

Let's talk categories: we love our categories, don't we? There are different ways to sort and categorize pretty much anything, including different ways to categorize food depending on your goals, needs, and preferences. A houschold with certain allergies will have very different food categories on their mind as they assess all the food on hand. Similarly, a change in job, family members, or location will all have an impact on how we see the organization and flow of funds through our budget kitchen.

When life, knowledge, and awareness or usage change, you may have to rearrange a bit. Some categories won't suit you in every stage of life. It's not open season to judge yourself or anyone else. You did what you did then, and each day you are choosing how to allocate and use resources based on what you know and need now and what is important to you.

Looking at the concept of categories is just that: looking, not a moral mandate on how to restock your pantry.

Sorting the sorting methods

There are several interrelated ways that people often categorize. Give each one a try now and then. Even if it doesn't become your go-to sorting method, each one can provide insights. The one (or ones) you choose to use will vary based on what is most useful to you in this season.

Method 1: Function served

One method of categorization is to batch categories by the function served in your life: with household items such as food and rent, then car and gas or transportation expenses, then perhaps also doing things outside of the house, such as dining out, entertainment, or travel.

Method 2: Fixed and variable expenses

Another categorization method is to separate out fixed and variable expenses. Fixed expenses always have to be there, and the price may also be fixed, like the cost of housing or insurance (for housing, transportation, or health). Not all fixed expenses will stay the same, and all prices change over the years. But in general, fixed expenses are either relatively constant, relatively predictable, or both.

Variable expenses fluctuate in amount and timing. This may be easy to determine, but sometimes there are things that are a bit in between. You always have to eat, but you have some choice about how you do so.

By tracking this over time, patterns may emerge. A utilities bill that falls on a certain day each month may vary each month. Even though prices change each year, the cost of heating and cooling may behave in certain relatively predictable ways around certain seasons.

Method 3: Needs versus Wants

You have almost certainly heard of one of the most typical ways to categorize: contrasting needs versus wants. Sometimes this feels very clear, such as deciding between a decadent chocolate cake or an ingredient for spaghetti sauce. Sometimes it is less clear, like a chocolate cake to celebrate an important milestone for a dear friend or loved one.

Method 4: But what is it FOUR, precious?

In her 2022 Morningstar article, Sarah Newcomb wrote, "After studying several theories of human motivation, I am convinced that we want things because we believe they will help us meet some deep need inside us." She advocates an understanding that our needs vary and that "we can turn budgeting into a creative problem-solving exercise that leads to deep fulfillment both in the present moment and in the future."

As an example from my young adulthood, most articles at the time were not decrying avocado toast but rather lattes and DVD rentals. Most budgeting advice I received (whether from people, articles, or blog posts) was all about cutting these two totally frivolous "wants" out entirely.

Newcomb argues that it is important not only to determine the underlying need but to measure whether the strategy for meeting that need is effective or efficient. My DVD rental was one of the cheapest options at the time that allowed me to combine entertainment and much needed rest after a long commute, without adding the full cost of movie purchases. Though all the blogs and advice railed against it, I chose the strategy that met a variety of my needs as cheaply as possible. What is important to you, for necessity, comfort, or connection? What are the strategies to fulfill these needs?

When you observe your cash flow, consider also the underlying need and urgency. If you are not pleased with the purchase, timing, or strategy you are using to meet that need, consider whether there is a different need in play. Maybe it is a conflict with your values or a more effective strategy. Take a moment to consider: When have you felt good about your choice for meeting that need? While a prior strategy may be an option that's no longer available to you, it could still inspire new ways that you could fulfill your needs gradually. Or you may realize that you were withholding a sense of fulfillment due to an expectation that no longer aligns with present circumstances.

As one of your Cooking Journal activities this week, you will make a list of categories for the ingredients in your life. There's no need to include any numbers yet; this is just seeing what ingredients are there. (This is also not about making changes today, although if there are scissors in the fork section, maybe just set those aside since that seems a bit too sharp to be in there.)

Most clients I work with want to make a change right away. Sometimes this is not because they actually want to, but because they think that is what is involved in this process. There are so many articles and content about what you need to change, do differently, cut back, or cut out entirely.

I assure you: just as arriving was a change and a practice last week, the change this week is in noticing and observing.

When clients come up with the list of categories, they often notice things about their income, expenses, spending, and values that they had not seen before. This is already a change. The categories we choose reflect our values, by revealing what matters to us to notice.

There are people for whom "Food" is a useful category. Others use two categories for food: "Groceries" and "Dining Out." A client who enjoyed nice restaurants wanted to pay attention to their fast-food dining in contrast with their preferred restaurant dining. Similarly, many people include a daily caffeinated beverage purchase in their Dining Out category, while others decide to have a separate category either out of concern that it is a larger expense than they'd like or because it is something important to them and they want to be sure to set aside funds for it.

While observing, one client noticed that they were spending a large amount on fresh flowers. Rather than deciding that this was a frivolous "want" to cut out, the client reflected on the experience of purchasing and having flowers. This client realized that having beautiful flowers in their space was extremely valuable for their well-being. Knowing this, they were able to make thoughtful decisions about their purchases, problem-solving how to ensure their home had beautiful arrangements. Some of the flowers could be longer-lasting, potted rather than cut, or positioned in a prominent or noticeable spot in the home.

As you go through the week, there are going to be times when you use or choose not to use money, resources, or skills to achieve what you hope for. This week, you are not trying to change any of these choices at all, merely observing and gathering some data.

If some needs are not being met by a strategy, do not despair. This is useful data. If we accidentally mislabel the information from a negative experience as if the information itself was negative, we may avoid the very information that could make our budget kitchen safer or more helpful for us. As we go through life, we will inevitably do things that either don't work perfectly or as expected. When this happens, remember you will only be able to use this important data next time if you gather it safely.

When you do something that can change your status quo, your inner critic (I.C.) takes that as a priority invitation to show up. Sometimes your I.C. will have something useful to say (even if it's coated with cruelty and lies), and sometimes your I.C. is just there to whine and worry you into the perceived safety of returning to the norm. That's ok. Change can be scary (and sometimes my inner critic shows up when I just need to rest).

Remember that I.C. voice is a visitor in the budget kitchen, but it is not the only one. Another guest is your Successful Self from the future. Mysterious but far from aloof, you can choose to invite a potential future self who is successful and grateful for your efforts, able to see clearly the path that brings you to that future.

As an antidote to your I.C., you can collaborate with your successful future self by asking "What would my Successful Self do?" (WWMSSD?) If that seems too big, recognize that your successful self knows the small steps that mattered for you to get there, and ask again. (And then do that little step.) Keep this tool in your toolbox and use it if you feel stuck or ashamed.

Remember: in the future, your successful self is grateful for what you are about to do right now to take care of yourself.

Action Step

For one week, simply notice. Write down any interaction with money or finances, whether interacting with a specific category or yearning for a future goal. Observe using whatever medium feels natural. When the inner critic arrives, ask: What Would My Successful Self Do?

Cooking Journal

Top 3 Priorities for the week ahead

1. What are you grateful for accomplishing last week?
2. What are your Top 3 Priorities this week? Write them down.
3. If a priority feels too big, break it into sub-tasks until one is completely doable today.
4. When there are a lot of tasks on the list, which are the three most important? What step can you take today? What must be done by next week?

Reflection Questions

1. Egg Timer Exercise

   Take a moment (as short as a two-minute egg timer) to list out as many possible categories in your budget kitchen. No classifying items, just naming categories and strategies. Here are 5 examples to start with or cross out. What comes to mind? Ready... Go!

   i. Housing

   ii. Food

iii. Fun
iv. Debt / obligations
v. Misc. / random

2. Considering Categories
   As you consider sorting methods (function, fixed and variable, needs and wants, needs and strategies), take a moment to ponder what it's all about. Not just money or stuff or spending, but also the deeper purpose and meaning in life. What is important to you, either for necessity or comfort or connection? What are the strategies to fulfill these needs? When have you felt good about your choice for meeting that need?

WWMSSD?

1. Successful Self vs. Inner Critic Exercise
   i. Your Inner Critic will show up throughout this process to scream and shame you away from things that either were or seemed dangerous in the past. It will notice things. Notice what it notices (and notice what's going on for you and your nourishment levels when your I.C. seems stronger, that little vampire). Just like with any pesky guest, you can tell your Inner Critic, "Thanks for sharing your thoughts, maybe go take a nap in the guest room."
   ii. By contrast: What would your Successful Self notice about your efforts this week?

iii. How does your Successful Self appreciate how you are setting yourself up for success this next week?

Week 3

Choosing Ingredients

"I don't really like numbers."

I have heard this more times than I can count and I have said it nearly as often.

I could not care less about the numbers themselves. To me, liking numbers is about the same as liking letters of the alphabet or an individual piece of uncooked spaghetti in the pantry. To me, it's all about the story. I like spreadsheets in the same way I like novels or art: I can appreciate their subject and composition, the way the information is presented to enhance narrative flow, how the lines and squiggles on the screen illustrate intention, evoke meaning, or give a window into a moment of reality.

You do not have to like numbers, spreadsheets, math, or letters of the alphabet to be here. Budget spaghetti is about crafting a cozy budget, designing a safe space from which to grow, and a comfortable feeling of home to return to. It's all about coming back daily to toss ingredients into the mix and throw some spaghetti at the wall to see what sticks. My past uncoordinated-child self would interject that a tasty spaghetti is also messy and fun.

Just as you eat each day, you also interact with the flow of money each day. You are practicing coming back regularly to notice when you have utilized your budget kitchen strategically, so that you begin to move from awareness towards empowerment.

Celebrate the noticing. Each time that you come back to your budget kitchen, you are building trust in your own self, not to be perfect or to know all there is to know (remember, that is simply not possible!) but to safely interact with this place of learning, experimentation, and growth.

This week, you will use the observations and practices from the prior weeks to begin to choose categories and ingredients. This involves both an awareness of what's in the pantry and of what you want to use today. Now that you've explored the ingredients and begun to puzzle out which ingredients matter to you, you can now begin to choose the ingredients with intention.

You're exploring what these ingredients represent, how (or whether) they support your joy, your identity, your energy, your goals. You will explore how those ingredients nourish you, provide fuel for your day, bring connection to those with whom you share the meal, and those who prepared the ingredients.

The way you perceive, categorize, and use these ingredients are connected with your values, needs, and intentions. Everyone will have different categories based on their own circumstances and preferred sorting method. A note of caution: If you're using the needs versus wants sorting method, take care not to sweep aside "wants" that may still have underlying unmet needs. If not addressed intentionally, these tend to pop back through as impulse purchases.

What's in the fridge?

Just like in the last chapter, we continue to notice things that are already here in the fridge: the categories of the items, the current flow of resources (including cash) through the household. As we set up, we need to reach in there and get some of those resources. If your kitchen (whether budget or culinary) is like mine, you may come across some things that you got at the grocery store some time ago, and perhaps also leftovers. As with any leftover resources, we need to check that it is still good and safe to use.

Let's go over a few things you know: You already eat, and you already manage your finances. What works well? What has felt successful in the past? Sometimes you can carry those successes forward. Sometimes (especially in lessons learned very young) you may realize with a compassionate chuckle that you have learned more since then.

Keep that compassion at the ready for the Noodle Exercise in this week's Cooking Journal. In your Cooking Journal, let all of the words flow out as they would with an excellent listener, not censoring or redirecting you at all, but always coming back to the kitchen safety guidelines, remembering to breathe, and coming back gradually to the questions and to the safety of the present moment. These reflections may have some good memories, some bad, some unusual, some that feel plain.

Take a deep breath in... and an even longer breath out. Even with some potentially questionable products in that pantry, there are sure to be some good, useful takeaways.

We're not running a chemical analysis on it, especially not that wannabe Tribble back there (wait, did that thing move?), but we do want to see where we are starting from. No matter what's there, you are here also. This is your budget kitchen, brave galactic warrior, and today is a good day to be right here, in this moment.

Cozy Categories

One of the most helpful strategies I've found for cozy budget categories has not been from a finance book, but from a book for ADHDers. In *Your Brain's Not Broken: Strategies for Navigating Your Emotions and Life with ADHD*, Dr. Tamara Rosier introduces her Solve-It Grid as an explanation of the types of task energies that can charge or deplete us. The Solve-It Grid is a four-quadrant chart spanning two axes: fun and level of emotion, with four quadrants (red, yellow, blue, and green). Use the information about the Solve-It Grid as you consider: What categories or items are the comfort food? What categories recharge?

The Solve-It Grid

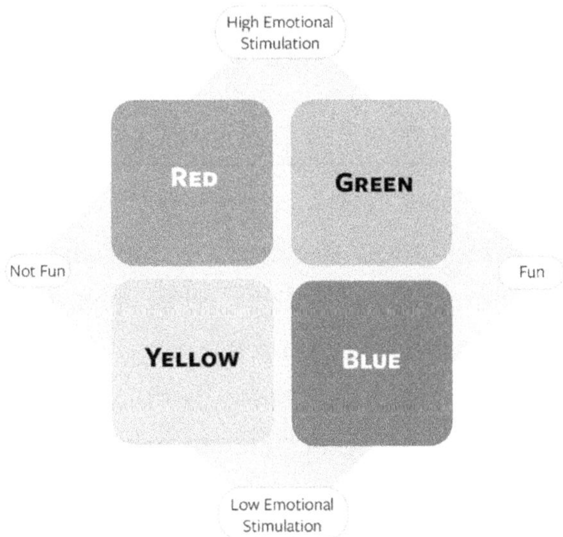

* *Excerpt from Your Brain's Not Broken by Tamara Rosier, copyright © 2021. Used by permission of Revell, a division of Baker Publishing Group.*

In the upper left, the Red Quadrant activities are highly emotionally stimulating and not fun. In the context of Dr. Rosier's work, these may be tasks or activities that have gained an emotional charge due simply to urgency, but which we can also maliciously amplify by procrastination, guilt, or shame. While these are highly depleting, we can get addicted to the frantic urgency and the dopamine boost from completing them. In my experience, the untended budget kitchen is on fire with Red Tasks, whether an annual birthday gift that didn't have funds set aside or bills with unknown, imminent, or overdue dates. Gradually, the goal is to turn down the burner on these and prepare a cozier cooking process with less fire danger.

In the lower left, the Yellow Quadrant activities are not fun and have low emotional stimulation. These can be the everyday routine activities that just get boring over time, or tasks with no set timeline. This is the budget kitchen of the status quo, the messes or recipes that are just there, like dozens of crock pots and pots kept on the back burner, slowly and steadily draining energy and increasing the fire hazard. Chipping away at some of these Yellow tasks or categories before they become Red can help increase the budget kitchen safety and preparation. As with boring, repetitive meal planning prep, I find that sometimes batching them or setting a timer can help get some of them done.

In the lower right, the Blue Quadrant also generates low emotional stimulation, but unlike Yellow, these activities are fun. These can recharge us, when used in moderation. Due to the low energy cost to do these tasks and knowing that they can be relaxing and recharging, we often choose these for rest or distraction from Red and Yellow tasks. Blue Quadrant can include activities like lying down for a moment or playing games on a screen. When used at the right amount for the time or circumstance, these activities slowly recharge us, but too long spent on a Blue task can become draining. And a "momentary" scroll or mobile game can end up depleting not only energy but bank balance through in-app purchases. It's important to spend some time in our Cooking Journal, but not so much that we avoid the cooking.

In the upper right, the Green Quadrant is fun and highly emotionally stimulating, recharging us quickly. However, Dr. Rosier notes that many of her clients either feel they don't deserve these or can't afford the energy startup cost to do these tasks. Being outdoors on a lovely day, even for a little bit, can be a Green activity for me. It feels like it will take so much energy, such a high startup cost despite the low monetary impact. But when I watch the sun's light fade or see the fog roll in, I am delighted and mesmerized, immediately recharged and enchanted. (And the price is nice!)

In various circumstances, certain types of purchases or actions may fall in different quadrants of the Solve-It Grid or may shift quadrants (especially Yellow to Red). What ingredient categories are comfortable and help us to thrive? These categories may tend towards the Blue or Green quadrant. Whether a chair that's comfortable but only for a limited time, remarkably lifelike fake plants, or looking out the window, items and activities fall in different quadrants on the Solve-It Grid.

Whether during the last few months or at any time, when have you decided how to use your existing resources to truly recharge? At some point, I think we all have seen ways in which at least one or two of the currently touted "self-care" options have a significant startup cost, whether in terms of money, space, time, or energy. Although in the right circumstances, these self-care options may be considered extravagant restorative experiences, in our day-to-day circumstances, these might actually deplete our limited resources without recharging our overall resource reserves enough to end up with a net positive outcome.

Even if energy is replenished, which with some of these things may simply not be the case for you in your own household reality, then it is worth noticing that the cost has been higher than we find comfortable.

In these cases, pause for a moment, not in judgment but in recognition: you are learning a valuable lesson about what strategies work (or don't work) for you in this time. This is useful information, and so even when you cannot recover the resources paid out, you can continue to benefit from the experience and recharge as much as we can from it, discarding and moving forward with gratitude.

A B.I.T. at a Time: The Budget Ingredients Table

The last two weeks, you have been exploring categories of inflow and outflow, especially when it comes to your money. You used a two-minute timer to brainstorm categories, and you kept the sorting methods in mind as you interacted with your budget kitchen over the last week.

The next step is to start putting things on the table, a bit at a time. Over the next month or so, your Cooking Journal will prompt you to fill in your Budget Ingredients Table. This chapter includes an example with the categories filled in as well as a blank B.I.T. for you to fill in.

Budget Category	Last Month (Actual)	This Month (Estimate)	Successful Self (Goal)
INFLOWS			
Primary income			
Other income			
TOTAL INCOME			
OUTFLOWS			
Housing / Rent / Mortgage			
Groceries			
Transportation			
Utilities			
Insurance			
Loan payments			
Maintenance (Housing/ Auto)			
Family / Child Care			
Entertainment / Subscriptions			
Dining out			
Personal / Fun			
Other wants			
Emergency fund			
Other savings			
TOTAL OUTFLOWS			
NET FLOW			
(Inflows minus Outflows)			

This week, you'll fill in the categories for your ingredients in the column on the left. As you fill in the categories column, you might choose to put the categories in order based on a particular sorting method (or label the categories with parentheses). It is your table, and you can always change the place settings later.

Remember, the rest will be filled out over the course of the next few weeks, so don't go overboard. Let's take this step-by-step together.

Action Step

Write in your categories on the Budget Ingredients table. Remember this is a no-judgment zone. If you're not sure about a particular category, write it down as you are thinking or feeling about it right now. You can always write it differently another time.

Budget Category	**Last Month (Actual)**	**This Month (Estimate)**	**Successful Self (Goal)**
INFLOWS			
TOTAL INCOME			
OUTFLOWS			
TOTAL OUTFLOWS			
NET FLOW			
(Inflows minus Outflows)			

Cooking Journal

Top 3 Priorities for the week ahead

1. What are you grateful for accomplishing last week?
2. What are your Top 3 Priorities this week? Write them down.
3. If a priority feels too big, break it into sub-tasks until one is completely doable today.
4. When there are a lot of tasks on the list, which are the three most important? What step can you take today? What must be done by next week?
5. Thinking of your Future Self of next week, what will you be grateful for accomplishing today?

Reflection Questions

1. Noodle Exercise

   Let's noodle over it: Set a timer for 10-12 minutes this time (about how long it takes for noodles to cook) and reflect:

   i. How did you first experience money, the budget kitchen of your youth? What do you want to keep from that? How do you want to grow from that? What is important to you?

   ii. Take the 10- to 12-minutes to reflect on these questions.

   iii. Return after the timer for reflection on what bits of all of that remain in the fridge right now. These reflections may have some good memories, some bad, some unusual, some that feel plain.

2. Enjoy and Be
   What's something you find simple or enjoyable to cook? Where do you find ease or efficiency in preparing for your day's well-being? As you go through this week, notice what you enjoy, what you want to emulate, when you make a decision that contributes to your financial sustenance. Remember: You can turn down the burner. You are safe to try things out or to just *be* here.

WWMSSD?

1. What elements of your budget kitchen do you imagine your future Successful Self will be grateful for? Consider how your Successful Self might be hoping to express gratitude and camaraderie as you clean, tidy, and set up your budget kitchen for the next day.

WEEK 4

Writing the Ingredient List

"Throw some spaghetti at the wall and see what sticks."

Like many people, I have said that classic cliché so often in so many contexts, including many times in and around my work. And like water over a temperamental stove, it finally came to temperature and brought together so many of my own thoughts, practices, studies, and experiences about money.

Like sticky spaghetti noodles you just can't get off the wall, once that phrase itself stuck, I kept noticing the connections to the metaphor everywhere in everyday life. It was as if the metaphor itself was on a slow simmer. Gradually, through brainstorming, experimentation, exploration, and revisions, it developed into a full, intentional approach to budgeting.

Last week, you began to think of categories for your cash flow. This week, you will begin to notice the overall composition of your cash flow.

The next step is a vulnerable one: gathering the data. From financial documents such as bank statements, credit card or loan statements, pay stubs, to the day-by-day experiences of cash inflow and outflow. All of the data will be useful data, even when (or perhaps especially when) we fear that it will not paint a picture we will be happy with. The value of this week comes from truthfully and vulnerably looking at the full picture, without judgment.

At the end of the chapter, you'll see an exercise for gathering it all into your Budget Ingredients Table. This may work for you if you're in a "get it all done and out of the way in one go" sort of Band-Aid-removal mood. But a budget is not a Band-Aid. It's perfectly fine to spend a moment here and there over a few days to just throw some numbers out there (a B.I.T. at a time) and see what sticks. That's what this is all about.

Grocery List

How do we make a grocery list? The first step is awareness that you are not starting something from scratch, but rather to recognize that you have already begun.

As you began to jot down notes and observations in your Cooking Journal, and especially as you curated categories the last couple of weeks, you have been bringing awareness to the inflows and outflows of your budget kitchen. Anyone who's had to make an actual grocery list (especially if there are multiple roommates or children involved) knows that one of the hardest parts of the grocery list process is knowing what's already in the pantry—and what anyone will actually eat.

It is one thing to think about categories of food or cash flow in theory, but it can be quite another to take a peek at how one's budgetary food pyramid is stacking up. Throughout this week, and going forward, stay curious. Stay observant. There will be items or even categories that you do not think of right away. That is a normal part of the process.

Remember that this approach is nonjudgmental and experimental. You don't have to know everything, but with some guidance you can give it a try and see what works. You can start with quick microwave meals to get basic calories and nutrition for the busy days, and over the next few months, you will get comfortable with using the metaphorical microwave, stove, oven, and whatever else your favorite recipes call for to make the budget feel like the cozy home you want to relax in.

Gradually, you will find that it is indeed possible to feel safe and cozy when thinking about and planning how to use money to attain your goals, whether imagining free-form or with guided prompts such as the Cooking Journal reflections or a recent bank statement.

Hunting and Gathering

Mechanically speaking, finding one statement or set of expenses is usually straightforward (whether the easiest is a bank or credit card statement or list of online purchases). Whether looking in a pantry, cabinet, or drawer, there's usually a spot that's easier to look than all the others. If you have ever found a sharp knife with the butter knives (hopefully not by way of the blade), you know that it can take a bit more effort to hunt for all the information you need, even if you thought you knew where you'd find it all.

Safety note: Always use the website or phone number on the back of your card and check for typos. Fraudulent websites, calls, or emails can be trickier to notice than that steak knife under the butter knives, so take the time and effort to maintain your kitchen safety practices and catch the misplacements where you can. If it catches you first, breathe. Turn down the stove. Reach out to an emergency resource from the back of the book. Get safe and take care.

Just like we had to seek out all the new life and civilizations lurking in hidden corners of the fridge or pantry, this week it's time to gather every financial document: bank, credit card, house or rent, loans, pay stubs. Even once you think you gather them all, one more statement or expense will almost always jump into the cart.

If you anticipate this happening and are thinking of postponing starting this task, you can do so. The task will still be here when you get back. Just know that the urge to avoid is completely normal. And still, you are capable and resilient. You keep coming back to this budget kitchen, and you are safe here. You are gathering all the data, without judgment. Your inner critic may show up, but I.C. can wait on the front sidewalk for this one.

For your Budget Ingredients Table, you only need the last full calendar month of data. However, if you're already hunting for that most recent month, you may be right near some additional helpful information. I recommend getting the last three months of all the financial statements, as not all expenses occur monthly. Digital or paper statements are fine, whatever you have and whatever feels most comfortable and helpful.

Make a list of any recurring bills or expenses. If you recall that there is an annual or irregular expense that has not happened in the last few months, jot down what you remember of it in your Cooking Journal anyway.

As you are hunting for this information, statements are not the only possible source of information. Thankfully, there may be some more modern tools available. Many banks and cards now offer spending reports online with visual breakdowns. While categories can be more generic and transactions may not be in the correct categories, spending reports can be a gentler entry point than raw statements.

Throw the Spaghetti

Once the documents are gathered and in one place, even alongside some possible overwhelm, most clients feel a sense of pride and relief. This is good. If you have been avoiding looking out of fear or shame, the act of bringing it all together is a huge accomplishment in itself.

It's time to imagine that putting that Budget Ingredients Table on a wall like a bizarre, budget-y pin the tail on the donkey party game. And get ready, because you are about to throw some spaghetti numbers at that first column.

It is not going to be neat and tidy. Maybe it won't have all the info or data the first time. But it is even better than perfect: it's a start.

The first numbers to throw are the income. Whether it's your main income, a second income, irregular income, small amounts, irregular amounts, or gifts, everything that flows in gets thrown on the B.I.T.

If you get a regular paycheck once or twice a month, throw it on the spaghetti wall and move forward. If you get a paycheck with the same dollar amount every two weeks, multiply it by 26 and divide by 12 to get your monthly inflow.

If your income amount varies but you get paid on a regular schedule, you'll need to use those last three months of data to get an average, possibly removing or discounting a larger inflow if you know it's not going to be typical (like those winter holiday season tips). If your income is only in select months of the year, you may find it more useful to look at the last year of inflows, averaging it out over 12 months (or even 13, to be more cautious).

Upon seeing the overall monthly income, some people feel relief, grief, surprise, or even bafflement at where it all goes. Whatever you feel, take a moment to pause. Notice. Breathe. Be present.

You've got this. And you got the data.

The next numbers to throw can be a bit messier: the outflows and expenses seen in the statements. This will include your usual expenses as well as those irregular ones: the filter replacement for the fridge or cat bowl, start of school year costs, the car washes when it's not rainy season, the higher or lower heat, air, or water bills depending on the season. As with the irregular or otherwise non-monthly inflows, you may wish to average irregular outflow categories using a few months of data or dividing it across all 12 months. Other outflows to account for (especially if you are self-employed) could include taxes, healthcare, additional saving for retirement.

If you're using spending reports, certain categories could be more ready to throw at the B.I.T., since the expenses are presorted into default categories. No matter what, remember that this is just the first month you're throwing this spaghetti. You will do it again next month (or, if you want to try on different categories, you could do so sooner).

Expect the Unexpected

Almost every budget will miss something unexpected. If you have a little wiggle room between inflows and outflows, keep some of that in a miscellaneous category for when that unexpected item shows up, even if it's just a few cents here and there. When that happens, know that it would've happened regardless, and now you can add it to your category list so that you are aware ahead of time. Sometimes you can already get ahead of things by thinking of some what-ifs pertaining to what you already have in your category list. For example, if you have a car, you know you will at some point need new tires.

For me, an interesting budget category to consider is clothing for work. Although I didn't always have disposable income to follow his advice, my dad would often recommend getting one clothing item for work every month or two. This kept his work attire fresh and didn't result in a huge clothing expense all at once. Dad, if you're reading this, I do appreciate the advice. Quite honestly, my biggest problem with following this advice is that I simply, truly, deeply, utterly loathe clothing shopping and would rather not do it. But even if I only spend it every so often, I can still mentally set aside funds for clothes as if I'm following my dad's advice.

The kitchen is now set up. The spaghetti is on the wall. It is time to breathe and reflect, maybe get a cup of tea by the budget kitchen window. As you notice your present self now compared with the beginning of the month, what changes do you already see? When have you noticed in the moment when you have made a decision that meets your needs in a way that feels good and healthy?

If you don't fill in the entire first column this week, that's ok. Keep gathering little by little each day. You've got this!

Action Step: Throughout the Week

Gather the most recent one to three months of financial data over the course of the week. Celebrate with a smile or gratitude from your Successful Self each time you gather a document throughout the week. You do not need to look at them right away.

Cooking Journal

Top 3 Priorities for the week ahead

1. What are you grateful for accomplishing last week?
2. What are your Top 3 Priorities this week? Write them down.
3. If a priority feels too big, break it into sub-tasks until one is completely doable today.
4. When there are a lot of tasks on the list, which are the three most important? What step can you take today? What must be done by next week?
5. Thinking of your Future Self of next week, what are (Future) You grateful for accomplishing today?

Reflection Questions

1. Home Sweet Home
   Where do your financial documents currently live? (Online, paper, various locations, unknown?) How good does your Successful Self feel to already have them gathered?

2. Inflow Reflection
   What are all the sources of income in your life right now? Does your income feel like enough? What comes up for you when you sit with that question?
3. Outflow Reflection
   Are your income or expenses relatively consistent from month to month or do they vary? If you live with greater variability, how do you stretch the leftovers when you have a bit extra?
4. Surprise!
   What surprised you when you filled in some numbers for the last few months for the Budget Ingredients Table? How does the data compare with what you expected to find?

WWMSSD?

1. Bring it on back to gratitude: no matter where you're at now, you are living a part of your Successful Self's success story. Even if you don't see the exact path forward, your Successful Self has lived it and knows that you will get there and will continue getting to new successes. WWMSSD to say thank you for what you have done this week?

Part 2

EXPERIMENT

It's the moment you've been preparing for!

You have practiced kitchen safety and built awareness of what you have on hand to work with, both in monetary resources as well as knowledge and past experiences. You have come back safely and calmly with increasing consistency. And you know (and perhaps even begin to believe) that you don't have to know everything about cooking to make a meal, nor do you have to know everything about money to practice using money and other resources for what you need.

In a world that implies we somehow "should" already know everything we need to know about money, it can seem uncomfortable to spend as much time as we have in a place of not knowing everything. But nobody will ever know everything. And remember: nobody has to. The whole point of Budget Spaghetti is experimentation. You find a recipe, you try it, you see if it tastes right. You figure out what you like and what you don't. You know that you don't have to know everything to have a good, delicious, cozy meal every day.

At the first stages in your budget spaghetti, you're not assuming you know the recipe, just some possible ingredients. Once you begin, you'll throw some of the ingredients you have into the pot, see how it tastes, and adjust as you go.

You already have a sense of some expenses and income, strategies and needs, desires and energy. And you have a comfort with some of these elements. Your Cooking Journal will be more important than ever. Just as if you were a mad scientist searching through experiment after experiment for the formula to some delightful brew, you will begin to experiment with what recipes work for your days, weeks, and months. You will continue to think through your values and stay attentive to your present self.

Observation often leads naturally to making small experimental changes. If you're like most people I've worked with, you may have noticed already that simply bringing awareness affected what you chose to do once or twice—or perhaps the decision felt different afterward.

In this section, you will make experimental changes. This is not the same as just making changes to try something different or new. When experimenting, we bring our curiosity about each element of the process and the calm conviction that even when we discover that the change has a different impact than we expected (whether for better or worse), this knowledge is worth having. Another key principle in conducting an experiment is to be sure not to change too many things at once. After all, if you get the result you were hoping for, you will want to know what specifically affected that result.

The experimentation process is truly a lifelong journey. As you experiment, the kitchen safety practices become even more important. Because the more you cook and experiment, the more your trials produce errors, all along the way to coziness. Gradually, you will develop an abiding appreciation for the experimentation process itself.

This involves finding moments of gratitude. To build your cozy budget, you will practice the essential habits of celebrating regularly and noticing the victories. Some of what works right now might not work in the future. The key is to stay present and find gratitude in the present moment.

Week 5

A Simple Spaghetti

This month, you will incorporate small experimental changes with a little action.

Remember, you have weeks of practice and experience looking at the overall budget kitchen from various perspectives, while keeping your kitchen safe. You notice what money strategies meet your needs, and you practice simply being in your budget kitchen every day. You bring your attention to the money moments with just as much care for your breath as to the steam rising from a cup of tea, watching the leaves move, or the cars drive by. In this moment, in this budget kitchen, you are here, and you are safe.

As you begin the simplest spaghetti, the challenge is keeping it simple. You have to keep it simple enough that you know you can rely on the flavors. If you begin to make a change, you will keep it so small that it is hardly noticeable most days. The simple spaghetti builds trust in the safety and comfort of the familiar, even as you weave in little changes towards a more robust, healthier meal down the road. This first week of experimentation is forming a hypothesis: what is the simplest spaghetti?

A simple meal provides a starting point. With a small number of ingredients and steps, you can find the reassurance this is enough for today. You can always figure out something different on another day. And that is how it is for your budget as well.

A simple meal can fulfill multiple needs at once: bodily sustenance, connection with people in the present or recipes from the past, an excuse to breathe in deeply to smell the sauce, the coziness of a homecooked meal for leftover lunch the next day. As you begin, you start with what you have. For simple spaghetti, you start with the water, noodles, and perhaps a jar of sauce. It must be clean water, it must be noodles that are safe for your body (if gluten must be avoided, for example), and a sauce that you will actually eat.

Similarly, as you read through this week, pick out just a few categories, and add a little more attention to the experience of each: from your existing knowledge and expectations to decisions about needs, quantities, strategies, and resulting experiences.

Now, talking about changes may have turned up the heat on the stove. So, let's pause for a moment, just to prove we can.

As you turn down the stove and breathe, imagine your thoughts are like a pot of water on the stove. What thoughts rise to the surface at this time? What changes have gone smoothly in the past, like water slowly rising to a boil, not too swiftly, not boiling over? What thoughts can rise and float away like the steam? And what item or category feels like it could be the simple spaghetti this week?

Counting Noodles

For me, one of the toughest parts of a simple spaghetti is the question of how much spaghetti is enough? I have a hard time believing the amount of dry spaghetti noodles, for many reasons: my grandma always made enough spaghetti for the entire family and then leftovers, my own household has hunger levels varying from hungry hobbits to already-ate-with-friends, and sometimes it's just that I poured a little fast and now a lot of broken noodle bits got steam on them so they might as well go in.

My dad, an analytical chemist, would often joke, "A pessimist says a glass is half empty, an optimist says the glass is half full, and a chemist says the glass is twice the size it needs to be." Well, quite the opposite of that chemist, anytime I make spaghetti, I end up with at least twice the noodles it needs to be.

This can happen while budgeting, too. Very often, when trying to find the perfect portion, you'll end up with a different amount than intended or expected when trying out your initial experiments. Store up all that knowledge in your Cooking Journal as you go.

How many spaghetti noodles (or your week's chosen ingredient) will be enough? Not for forever, but for today? What have you already got? Have you checked all the usual places? What about unusual places or strategies? Consider all of those creative shelving strategies you're practically guaranteed to find after you get back from the grocery store.

Think of the noodles as a category or item of expenses; the metaphorical pot they're cooked in is the income or cash flow available. Overall, your cash available has to be large enough for your expenses to fit inside. Like noodles, some expenses can seem at first like they'll take up a certain amount of space, and then they expand.

If you begin to notice that your expenses are greater than the income or are expanding too quickly, that's useful information. Breathe, and remember the emergency resources at the back of the book are there if you need them. You are not alone, and you are capable of getting to a safer place.

You might end up pouring different amounts each day that you cook spaghetti, and you may similarly notice you are pouring different amounts each day for a budget category you're observing this week. Maintain gratitude as you observe. This information is useful to know.

With the water boiling and the noodles added, you can heat up the sauce in another pan. For a simple spaghetti, the jar of spaghetti sauce from the store can be awesome sauce. Check that you're not wearing something that could be ruined by a drop of sauce, pour the sauce in, and heat it up.

You made money choices in your budget kitchen, and you made budget spaghetti! You took note of the amount and process. You are setting yourself up for nourishment next time. You are bringing your existing skills into your own unique budget process and strengthening your skills and habits.

Notice What Matters

Do you know the feeling of biting off more than you can chew? I do it all the time, even when I think I won't. This time, the idea really is simple, I say to myself. I'll just pick up a couple items from the floor of my closet. Next thing you know, the cat is cartwheeling through a mess of scarves or something else I'll never wear as my entire wardrobe is scattered on the floor.

The trick (and it really is a tricky one!) is to discern what matters. Sometimes you'll pay attention in the moment but really understanding what matters about it will come later. If things get overwhelming, recenter on those questions from the top 3 priorities habit: What is it that matters here? What is the hope or the intent? What is either the ideal amount to do or the minimum next step?

As a society, we tend to praise those who are or appear to be doing more than possible. But let's do a reframe: if something is challenging and you come back to it, you are doing more than you thought might be possible. If you began thinking that you couldn't do numbers or money, and you realize that you spend a few minutes in your budget kitchen checking out what's there and what you might need on hand this month, that is you doing more than you thought was possible. Congratulations! You do hard things every day.

If you set out to do more than could ever be possible in a single day, more than likely you will not succeed; but if you set out to do the next possible (albeit difficult) step towards what matters, you may find that you are already doing more than you realize, and that you can build on these successes towards your Successful Self.

With that in mind, set aside a few 10- to 12-minute noodle timers this week to do a B.I.T. at a time filling in the first two columns of the Budget Ingredients Table. Estimate what it would actually be this month, without any changes in choices or patterns. The ultimate goal here is to have a middle column that reflects the current reality.

Pay particular attention to one category at a time, as well as any connections with needs, strategies, values, or goals. How does the category nourish? Is it as filling as you thought it would be, and does it satisfy? If not, is there another need or strategy to test out tomorrow?

Keep checking in on that breathing automation; you may find a few glitches or hiccups at this stage. Jot it all down in your Cooking Journal: the amounts, the breath, the experience, the energy flow. What do you notice? What do you hope? What brings you joy? When you pour the amount of noodles you intended, celebrate! When the sauce is a bit much or not quite the right type or flavor, acknowledge your experience and add a dash of gratitude for what you've learned.

Continue to incorporate the reflections: What have you learned for next time? What do you appreciate about your developing process? Where might you eventually be comfortable adding a little complexity, a little more than the simplest of spaghettis?

Action Step

As you sort that gathered data into your pantry ingredient categories, put an estimate for what this month's amounts will be based on that past information.

Notice how the estimate feels. Are you tempted to write a different number than the previous data shows? What hopes or fears are simmering under the surface?

Tell yourself: I am doing my best. I take care of what I can. I am able to breathe, learn, and grow.

Cooking Journal

Top 3 Priorities for the week ahead

1. You are a third of the way through.
   i. Last month, how amazing are you for arriving as often as you did?
   ii. What are you grateful for accomplishing last month?
2. What are your Top 3 Priorities this week? Write them down.
3. Break things into subtasks if they're big. Which items are your priorities this week? Which items will be a priority for Future You?
4. What are You (of next week) grateful for accomplishing today to take good care of yourself?

Reflection Questions

1. Spaghetti Sauce and Awesome Sauce
   You made a meal! You made a day that had money choices. You made budget spaghetti. Does it feel like you made a good amount for what you need today? What have you learned for next time? What do you appreciate about your process? Where did you experience complexity sneaking into your simplest spaghetti?
2. A Little More Attention
   Pick out one or two categories or items and just add a little more attention to the experience of this item: the decisions, the feelings, the needs, the strategies. For each category or item this

week, when you choose an amount, what do you expect or anticipate about this amount? When the amount is either just right, too much, or too little, what is the next strategy you choose?

WWMSSD?

1. If you were tempted to write a different number for a category, pencil it in for the third column. Your Successful Self may have that number on their regular monthly list. Write a letter from your Successful Self to your present self, urging you to be patient and consistent. The work that you are doing right now is a part of your success story.

Week 6

Add Some Spices!

Think about your favorite comfort food: the memories, the flavors.

It may be a rich, slow-simmered pasta sauce, a comforting broth made with love, or a perfectly balanced mac and cheese.

For me, despite what this book's title may suggest, my favorite comfort food is a slow-cooked pot roast on a chilly day, the kind that may not have a lot of ingredients or spices. With only a little prep work or effort, the slow cooker has been doing all the cooking work for me all day. As I walk in the door with the outside air wafting into the room, the flavor of warmth is already on the air. As I breathe in through my (possibly stuffy) nose, the chill of the day shakes itself away from my bones and I'm filled with the peace of *home*, even before taking a bite.

Any chores are immediately infused with the fragrant certainty of a tasty meal. Whenever the exhaustion of the day seeps in, so too does the smell of that hearty roast, made with relatively little and yet bursting with flavor. Memories arise of experiencing it for the first time, making it out of habit when I'd moved out on my own, preparing it for my family, and making it purely for myself and for my own comfort.

The best meals aren't just about ingredients; they're about how they make you feel. So it can be in many areas of our lives, and money is no exception. Some income or spending feels amazing through and through, some feels just neutral, and some brings an unpleasant aftertaste or discomfort whether now or in the future.

As you keep making the food that nourishes you, it's time to adjust the flavor. For spaghetti, this may involve following a recipe or suggestion at the beginning of creating the sauce and then tasting it after it simmers a bit. When you taste the sauce, you notice what's already there: the tomatoes, oregano, garlic, pepper, salt, and so forth. My grandma's recipe had so many delicious flavors, from the garlic to the ground beef. And it had celery. Why celery? Welcome to the most baffling culinary question of my childhood. Thankfully, my grandma was willing to cut back on the celery when she made the recipe for us.

This week, as you make your spaghetti sauce each day and think of adding some flavor, you may also notice what is not there. Would it make the sauce better to have it or leave it out? This takes a lot of trial and error, all of which will become either delicious nutritious meals or data points on the way to success.

Salt, Pepper, and Cayenne Pepper

Beyond the core expenses in each category, the spices you use in the budget kitchen reflect how these money choices are uniquely yours.

In a sauce, adjusting the flavor or spices can result in anything from delicious to bland or even gag-reflex territory, or anything in between. Sometimes, you can get one of these experiences from the way you approach a particular category of outflows. Looking at the category of streaming services, for example, you may realize that it's not even that the dollar amount is too much, but that the time spent watching is not recharging you enough in this season.

Sometimes, as with veggies for my younger self, a little bit of that gag reflex was nonnegotiable for sufficient nourishment. Some expenses are like that too. It's not the most pleasant, but maybe eventually there are ways to make it a little less unpleasant. My go-to veggie strategy as a young adult out of college was to smother it in teriyaki sauce.

Let's say after a taste of a spaghetti sauce, you suppose that it could need a bit more salt or pepper. To test this hypothesis, you add some pepper. You may be extra careful not to put too much, because sometimes even a small amount can make a big change. With saltiness, too much or too little can make or break the recipe, but also everyone's got different opinions and health needs. I have vast experience with turning a reasonable amount of food into a feast with days of leftovers due to a fast-pouring pepper shaker.

Or there's the situation in my house with cayenne pepper. It all started when I followed a recipe years ago that had cayenne pepper. My spouse and stepkids thought it was fine, just some mild flavor. Meanwhile, for me, it was so spicy I could barely breathe and needed constant sips of milk to even make it through a small helping. Over time and through many experimental recipes, I gradually realized it's not that I can't handle any spiciness at all (as the kids like to joke), but just that I could *not* handle cayenne pepper. And that's ok; they can add more of their own if they want to. I can still make the meal with some seasoning (with the tiniest fraction of a pinch of cayenne pepper) that we all supplement with other seasonings according to our tastes.

You have that same ability with your own finances. The ingredients, spices, amounts, proportions that work great for someone else's budget spaghetti will not always align with yours, but with a base recipe, you can make modifications as you serve your own dish.

This week, notice the way you use flavor in your budget kitchen. What is the salt or sugar that may be best in moderation? What is the cayenne pepper in your ingredients list? Notice when shame or stress overpower the recipe. Breathe. Adjust or accept for the day. Notice also when excitement or urgency leads to shortcuts, and whether those shortcuts diminish the flavor or enhance the overall experience. Every day, consider how you can throw in a little compassion to balance it out as you spice intentionally.

Cooking through Uncertainty

Have you ever avoided looking at a planner or to-do list because you think there's too much to do and you're not sure how it could possibly all get done?

Rather than facing reality, perhaps you look at a book, movie, or doom scroll, but that underlying worry is still there, building its way up the ladder towards fear. The longer that fear simmers, the less time there is to complete the to-do list.

If you know the list needs to be done and are unsure if it can be done in the allotted time, the first step is to be in the fear. Bring breath and attention to the feeling. The next step is to be present, to listen and react appropriately to what the fear is trying to tell you. And no, I don't know what the fear is trying to tell you, but I do know that you have been doing very well at practicing listening to yourself. You know more than you think you do.

When you allow yourself to look and notice the fear, you can then also look towards the strategies or tiny adjustments that could help you get around the obstacle, either this time or the next.

You learn from the days you show up, and you learn from the days you scroll away. It's how you use what you learn that matters. You are learning that the times you don't get it "perfect" are just data points in your Cooking Journal, steps in the larger recipe to learn from as you move forward. It's all just a part of the journey to getting a better result next time.

The Seasoning for the Season

This week as you observe your budget spaghetti, notice also the emotional flavor palates of spending and earning. How does this blend together or interact with the energy of the day, or with the preparation, the product, the setting? In observing the emotional flavors, you are still not judging them as good or bad. Instead, you are noticing which budget kitchen actions this week result in a robust, full-flavored meal, perhaps with coziness, nostalgia, or just the "chef's kiss" amount of all spices and flavors.

As you notice spending or earning, which items or categories have a gag reflex or, like me with cayenne pepper, cause you to reach with urgency for milk or bread or some other way to cope? If the item must still be included (like vegetables), what strategies do you implement already to mitigate the effects? Chances are, you already use some. When have these strategies worked well? Which items or actions solve the problem by default, just by having them on hand when needed? What options are there for next time? For example, a mango lassi, had I known ahead of time of my cayenne reaction, would've been a beautifully refreshing pairing with the dish.

There will also be bland income and expenses. Some work well that way: a water bill or a routine car maintenance check are definitely dishes best served bland. As you notice any bland items or combinations, observe and take note. Do they work well that way? Do they ever seem to have a different flavor or impact? Noticing these contrasts can help to bring awareness to the surrounding circumstances and factors in our budget kitchen. Our whole experience affects not only the bland moments but more flavorful moments as well.

For example, the same large grocery order can feel like an accomplishment one day but overwhelming on another, depending on how rested I am going into the store. Circumstances and environmental factors can change the flavor, even when the quantities and composition seem identical. Consider how you use all of your resources (whether financial, emotional, relational) in support of your well-being. The amount of a resource needed on any given day isn't just about the overall total nutrients, but about the flavors that make it delicious (or make us gag).

Return to the overall goal. You are building appreciation for the process of testing things out, observing, and learning. You are bringing new knowledge and experience to the budget kitchen process. You are keeping that curiosity and growth mindset as you come back again and again. Coming back is the win.

Action Step

Pick out just one category that you use on a regular basis. Make a point each day to decide how much or little of it you are using, and how you are seasoning it. Take note of your experience. If it gives you a gag reflex one day, that's data for the next day. If it's not enough one day, that's data for tomorrow. If it's too much or just not needed or thought of on another day, that's useful to recognize, too. Notice how even the same exact recipe doesn't always hit exactly the same each day.

Cooking Journal

Top 3 Priorities for the week ahead

1. What are you grateful for accomplishing last week?
2. What are your Top 3 Priorities this week? Write them down.
3. Break things into subtasks if they're big. Which items are your priorities this week? Which items will be a priority for Future You?
4. What are You (of next week) grateful for accomplishing today to take good care of yourself?

Reflection Questions

1. Energy Exchange
   How do the ingredients for your needs and nourishment blend together or interact with the energy of the day? As you observe the emotional

flavors, which budget kitchen actions this week rcsult in a robust, full flavor?

2. It's the Consistency
   Which spending or earning have a gag reflex or cause you to reach with urgency for some other way to cope? If it must still be included, what strategies do you implement already to mitigate the effects? Are those strategies working and helpful, or are they on hand? What other possible options are there?
3. Balancing Bland
   Which income and expenses are bland in flavor? Do they work well that way? Do they ever seem to have a different flavor? How can you use the contrast between bland or spicy to bring awareness to the broader circumstances in your budget kitchen experience? How do you factor that in with intention to balance the bland and flavorful moments?

WWMSSD?

1. As you go through these cooking experiments, some of the results will feel like a waste. Your Successful Self is here with you, remembering well your frustration, disappointment, or fear. Wherever you are at now, your future Successful Self knows that you will get through it.

WEEK 7

Once More, On Purpose

You have done so much in these last six weeks. You arrived at the budget kitchen and learned how to be present safely and compassionately.

Some of this compassion comes from noticing that just as you decide how to provide yourself with food to nourish you each day, you also decide how to provide yourself a nourishing money experience. You are moving from thinking and preparing towards action, and this week is all about using that action and momentum on purpose.

The goal is to keep returning to what works for the season, ultimately finding the habits and community that will support you in your lifelong budget kitchen journey.

Crafting a Familiar Recipe

You already make budget spaghetti. You have thrown the numbers onto the spaghetti wall and recorded the results in your cooking journal, and you have seen these numbers shift and fluctuate at times.

What do you notice in exploring the flavor palate of your usual daily budgetary recipes? Have you found little things you enjoy sprinkling in, like a dash of cinnamon in a hot apple cider? Perhaps a bit more garlic in the spaghetti sauce, or removing the celery from the recipe and just adding a vegetable on the side?

Having reflected on the flavors that you enjoy and that bring you comfort, it is time to practice making those little shifts on purpose. When you practice these tiny recipe changes and check if they work in differing conditions, this is all still a part of your Successful Self's success story. Regularly recognizing how you are actually doing the thing can make the next mindset shift from "I already do it to survive" to "Now, when I am in a safe space, I know I can start doing things on purpose to prepare and enjoy the flavor."

Honing a Craft

This book is about crafting: exploring, being, envisioning, and ultimately, creating.

In crafts as varied as crochet, music, design, or sports, you learn some basic skills, practice them, try them in different circumstances, see how they work, learn more detailed skills or versions of skills, and repeat the process.

Now that you've seen how you already make budget spaghetti, and now that you've had some small spice experiments, you can notice the elements of the craft as you're going about daily life. Much like my friend pauses to look at woodworking or a musician who hears and appreciates techniques of a song being played, you also are beginning to notice, perhaps with wonder and admiration, the choices in all of the myriad crafts that surround us every day, including crafting a budget.

As with a particularly complex crocheted sweater pattern, recognize that you are working to meet your needs while continuing to learn and practice what helps hone your craft.

In crochet, it is the steady pattern of learning, practice, and implementation, that builds layer upon layer, row after row. The simple stitches for a quick scarf can become relaxing, even a meditation in movement that brings calm to the day through the familiar repetition. So it is with your craft of budgeting.

This week, find familiarity in the rhythm of the noticing. Where have you also felt comfort seep into the process? Do you celebrate when you choose something cozy or that supports yourself in the future? It may be a grocery list, planning a meal for tomorrow, or choosing to grab a basket (skip the cart!) to make it happen. How do you express gratitude and recognize your choice?

Each day, weave in the gratitude for the efforts that got you here, even as you choose to discard methods that no longer work for your current stage of the craft.

The Allure of Automation

Putting together ingredients with intention, planning ahead, and even just repeating the experiment the next day are all part of the continued success. The key is to nourish now, learn, and give yourself permission for next time to be different as you grow. You are making progress just by being here, just by noticing your experience in this moment.

By this point in your journey, you may have done a budget kitchen pantry check on autopilot, or you have begun breathing more deeply before you're even aware you were beginning to feel stress or anxiety. The steps are becoming part of the flow, indistinguishable from all of the other steps of the day.

Along the way, you will wonder how much more you could accomplish if you could automate. Of course, certain things can be automated. For example, I'm very glad to find that I am breathing (at least shallowly) whether I am thinking about it or not! And there are ways to automate elements of budgeting, whether by spending reports or using a budget app that automatically tracks expenses.

We all bring our values, our hopes, and our dreams into how we interact, even with something as seemingly simple as a spending report graph. The categories and ingredients in a default plan have a different flavor than those that we select on purpose for our own goals and dreams.

And more importantly, remember that most basic definition of a budget: it is a plan. And your Successful Self's cozy budget is not just A Plan, but Your Plan. For a plan to remain yours even as your life and experiences change, it is your awareness and your intentions that will bring it back into alignment, so it can never fully automate.

Finding the Right Balance

When I was budget coaching, many of my clients came to me wondering: at the end of the day, week, or month, where did all those inflows go?

Many clients knew certain category amounts like housing or the monthly phone or internet bill, but those were nowhere near the total amount that seemed to be flowing out each month. After a few sessions of accumulating observations and data, I would often ask: Is there a leak, an unexpected outflow? Usually, the answer was yes. The next question: Is it a slow and steady leak, or is it a one-time huge, gushing leak?

People would find all sorts of leaks. Sometimes, they had a slight awareness of what this would be: books, comics, games, tea, or coffee. Sometimes they found things that reflected their values, but which they had not accounted or planned for. These included: donating money, food, lightly used clothing, or furniture, and then replenishing regularly; buying food locally, organic, or without preservatives; buying beautiful yarn, flowers, or extra comfy blankets and pillows; having cash on hand to buy a meal for someone; tipping generously to brighten someone's day.

Even when something starts out as a leak, it doesn't have to remain that way. Once you name that underlying need or value, I assure you that you can make a conscious choice.

It's like if your water bill suddenly seems unmanageable. You don't just say, "Oh, well. No more using water." If you have your previous bills, you can see what the flow has been before. You might discover that the underlying price went up. Or perhaps your total bill went up because a relative moved back in for the summer and the consumption went up. Or you can discover that you actually have a running toilet or other leak. (Raise your hand if you've discovered the latter by way of a water bill...)

Sometimes the leak in our budget is simply inflation or a costlier season of life, but sometimes there is an unexpected leak. Sometimes it's a small, steady leak. Other times, it's a water main. Awareness of the flow helps you identify the strategy you'll need to use to be able to repair, address, or maintain it in a way that is either fully or incrementally more aligned with your values day by day.

Explore the Intention

Just as identifying leaks isn't just about the numbers, this week, you will explore your intentions for the categories in the Budget Ingredients Table. This helps not only in bringing awareness to the little experiments in the present but also with preparing to fill in the Successful Self's column next week.

First, copy down your categories. Instead of the other three columns with numbers, this time you'll have four columns of questions. The first question is: What do I want? Next, address the question of: What underlying need(s) does this address? Third, jot a few notes on the question: What does this reflect about my values? And finally, consider: How do (or can) I use this on purpose?

Action Step

Fill in some answers in your Intentional Ingredients Table categories. For each row, write something in the needs and/or values columns, even just one word. Pick a category you want to honor and decide how you will approach it this week with intention and purpose.

Category	What do I want?	Underlying need(s)	Value(s) reflected	How will I use this on purpose?

Cooking Journal

Top 3 Priorities for the week ahead

1. What are you grateful for accomplishing last week?
2. What are your Top 3 Priorities this week? Write them down.
3. Break things into subtasks if they're big. Which items are your priorities this week? Which items will be a priority for Future You?
4. What are You (of next week) grateful for accomplishing today to take good care of yourself?

Reflection Questions

1. Well, That Was Unexpected...
   You have been observing and experimenting for nearly two months now. What have you found that is unexpected? Describe an experience when noticing something has helped you realize a small adjustment that could help.
2. Celebrating the Cozy Comforts
   Where have you also felt comfort seep into the process? How do you celebrate when you choose something cozy or that supports yourself in the future?

WWMSSD?

1. As you fill in some of the Intentions questions related to your budget ingredients, where do you feel the support of your Successful Self? What delicious, flavorful categories are currently a little bland, but your Successful Self knows the flavor will develop over time? What items are like cayenne pepper, but your Successful Self can handle the heat better or decides not to use as much?

WEEK 8

Your Cozy Recipe

For the last two months, you have been practicing in this budget kitchen.

You found and held this space. You built and designed a place to let the breath flow and the hopes percolate, where essential nutrition blends with the strategies for value attainment. In practicing and expanding on the simple spaghetti, you are developing the foundational skills that will serve you anytime you return to the craft, whether today, tomorrow, or in the future.

Hopefully, you have already found the coziness in breath, presence, and awareness in a small flavor success from one of last week's spice adjustments.

This week, to wrap up the month, I invite you to consider the life and values of that Successful Self you yearn to emulate and become. Seek out the smallest meaningful ways to prepare the budget kitchen for that Successful Self, and therefore also for your near-future self.

This is admittedly a very tough one to write about. By definition, this will be something deeply personal, perhaps unknown even to you at the start of this week. How then could I hope to write about it? In truth, I cannot.

Instead, I can share an example of how such a mindset shift can unfold. This is how it happened for me, but it will happen differently for you.

The Chai Challenge

When I was younger, I had two categories pulling me in what felt like opposing directions. Like a game of tug of war, each day felt like there could be only one winner or loser, and no matter what, there was a loss or a lack. Strangely enough, these two clashing categories led to the intentional reframes that built up my own financial empowerment. To begin with, I should say that my total outflows were always less than my inflows. The description that follows is a tug of war between two possible ways to use additional cash flow.

I began budgeting at my dad's instruction when I was in second grade. Although I rebelled against it as I grew up, I always had it as something I could fall back on as a practice. But the budget of a child with a tiny allowance, with required saving and giving, and only wanting paperback books is very different from that of a young adult with college loans, rent, food, transportation, other expenses, and a very long commute.

As a young adult, my budget kitchen journey began with an impulsive daily chai on the way to work.

When I was working at a job that required a long commute and which left me exhausted and drained each day, I would frequently get myself a cozy chai on the way to work. It served multiple functions: the caffeine helped keep me more alert on my long commute, the flavors brought me joy and comfort, and I started my day with my hope feeling a little less depleted. It happened so often that I noticed it adding up. It didn't even seem to matter if I decided not to the night before or as I got into my car. After several minutes of driving, I would still find myself standing in line at the little coffee shop near the freeway.

On the other side of the tug of war loomed my student loans. A leviathan of debt that was slow-moving and equally crushing. Even the income-based monthly payments weighed in at a much greater dollar amount than my morning chai. In charting the realm of achievements, these felt off the map. I knew if I paid only the interest, I would never even make a dent in them, and so I did sometimes make an extra payment, whether part of a large gift or unexpected savings. Nonetheless it felt like shoveling a mountain with a teaspoon.

Logically, I knew that if I had fewer chai lattes, I would have more left at the end of the month to dedicate to diminishing the student loans. Try as I might, even wanting in theory to budget or stick to a plan did not translate to the desired action when it came to making the purchases.

I figured I just lacked discipline and willpower.

But I wasn't going to let that stop me.

I don't know how many weeks it took me to realize that it did not matter when I decided not to have the chai; it mattered whether I decided to get into the left turn lane to get to the coffee shop. That decision was sometimes made within a few feet of the turn lane opening up. Some days, I could then avoid the chai by getting into the furthest right lane earlier, but it was not consistent. The chai tasted like freedom before an hour of rush hour drudgery and a full day of work.

Once I realized the decision point, I had to reframe the decision. If I was deciding between chai or no chai, then chai would be the tastier option. If I was deciding between the comfort of a chai and paying off my student loans, then one was tangible and imminent while the other seemed impossibly distant.

But what if I decided between paying then-$4 (rounded up) for the chai or something comparable in price? I resolved to let myself decide each day whether I wanted to spend $4 on the chai or pay $4 toward my student loans. If I chose the student loans, I paid the $4 as soon as I got to work, or at least by my lunch break. After all, if I'd bought the chai, then I figured that the money would be out of my account already too.

I expected that this would practically eliminate my chai expenses, bringing logic and order into a chaotic, emotional, irrational decision. I was raised solidly in the needs versus wants sorting method, so I fully expected to find that this chai was entirely useless, a waste, a mistake, and one that I kept making but could stop if I only were clever or determined enough.

To my surprise, I discovered that the chai was not just the frivolous want leeching away at any hopes of long-term happiness that I'd thought it had been. On the days when I found myself in line waiting for the chai, I began to notice that I felt a bit better about the impending start to my workday, a little more capable of rising to meet the soul-numbing tasks ahead of me. I felt more joy and hope and happiness.

When doubt or shame crept in, of course these positive benefits were severely diminished. Therefore, on those days that I chose chai, I reasoned that I had to not only be willing to pay the $4 but also allow myself to fully enjoy it, otherwise that $4 was indeed wasted. Sometimes I still felt guilty, but I would remind myself intentionally each time that happened: if the purpose of the purchase was to make me feel happier and have a relaxing focal point of my morning, then to feel guilty would negate that purpose.

No matter what I chose, I reminded myself each day that I could make a new decision tomorrow.

For that day, if I had decided to enjoy a chai, then I did. If I decided that I didn't really want to spend anything because I had another expense coming up or wanted to build my cash buffer, I enjoyed that decision. And then I enjoyed it again later when I had more ready for that other expense or if something came up. If I decided to pay towards my student loans, then I not only paid a little towards my student loan, but I also filled in a little spreadsheet I made that showed how paying down the principal was decreasing the amount of interest I had to pay each day, even if only by a few cents at a time.

Little by little, the $4 student loan payments paid a bit more principal, the chai tasted better, the month's spending felt more comfortable. So gradually that I didn't even notice the mindset change, through this intentional enjoyment and affirmation of this daily decision, I somehow found that I had confidence in my own financial choices.

This confidence became palpable not just in that morning commute moment, but throughout the days, weeks, and months. Even so, for years, I saw this more as a way to trick my brain, as if my own present self was an adversary to outwit.

Over time, I began to frame it more as noticing a potential hazard or stumbling block on a common road and finding the strategy to navigate it over time.

Sometimes, it's not enough to have the cozy result, like sipping a chai, even when the coziness was a desired outcome. The way you choose the coziness must be cozy on purpose as well, finding the decision point that allows the tug of war to move not just in opposition but forward together toward both goals.

That is the recipe you are learning to craft in your budget kitchen.

Revise a B.I.T.

As you experiment with the recipe, you make it yours, trying little adjustments and enhancements to see what flavors and ingredients make the sauce taste better to you in each season.

You are transforming your recipe from a rough but workable first draft to a living document draft, like a recipe handed down with multiple generations of notes and adjustments in the margins. Each day, you are finding ways to infuse the resulting awesome sauce with coziness.

In honor of this working, living recipe draft, it is time now to return to the Budget Ingredients Table. Before looking at the third column, the realm of the Successful Self, let's look back at the estimates for this month. What is this month at now? What turned out as expected and what went differently? Based on this knowledge, how would you write next month?

No matter the answers, be sure to observe safely, finding compassion without complacency. Next month is a new month, filled with days like today and tomorrow. Each day has choices you make, needs to fulfill, new information to observe and collect.

While you consider the next month, continue to notice where your future Successful Self would see some similarities and differences on their column of the Budget Ingredients Table. Jot them down in the column on the far right. Start with the gag reflex ingredients to get them out of the way. Consider how your Successful Self might have learned to either tolerate or incorporate those categories with something better tasting. Continue on to the saltiest, spiciest ingredients, those ingredients which have the sharpest, most noticeable flavors, and ponder how your Successful Self might utilize them, or what alternatives you may have for meeting needs. Continue until even the blandest of categories are filled in.

Overall, the Budget Ingredients Table of your Successful Self may look rather similar in some areas and quite different in others. Perhaps instead of student loans, you imagine your Successful Self will be done with those and saving for retirement, home improvements, family care, or travels. Some elements may be replaced or substituted, while others may be a similar or smaller proportion of your income.

As you nudge your next month towards that possible future recipe with small, consistent flavor choices each day, continue to make note over time of what has worked and what doesn't work. These notes are not necessarily a GPS map with a countdown timer, but are more like a compass, revealing a possible direction pulling on that category.

Action Step

Go back to your Budget Ingredients Table. Update at least two categories to reflect what you have learned in the last few weeks. Make some flavor notes of what you learned so that your future self can decide how to incorporate the category cooking notes. Cooking involves experimentation, and when you make note of an experiment, you can have that data on hand for the next cooking experiments!

Cooking Journal

Top 3 Priorities for the week ahead

1. What are you grateful for accomplishing last week?
2. What are your Top 3 Priorities this week? Write them down.
3. Break things into subtasks if they're big. Which items are your priorities this week? Which items will be a priority for Future You?
4. What are You (of next week) grateful for accomplishing today to take good care of yourself?

Reflection Questions

1. Chai Challenge, Your Edition
   What would your version of the chai challenge be? What element of enjoyment for your present feels at odds or in opposition with some future goal? How can you find a way to turn those

opposing flavors towards balance over time? How do you already take good care of your future self now?

WWMSSD?

1. After revising a B.I.T. of the present month, invite your Successful Self to fill out the Budget Ingredients Table, column 3. As you look at it, this may feel totally impossible or aspirational in some areas. Write it down anyway. You can always write something different tomorrow.

Part 3

SUSTAIN

Breathe.

You have done so much as you have learned the foundations of this cozy craft. Recall how you have practiced arriving, noticing, and setting up the ingredients you have. You have experienced the flavors and energy of cash flow each day and have become more comfortable with experimenting with the strategies you use to meet your needs.

You have come back repeatedly to your present self. You can remind yourself to notice when you circle back to the present moment. You are aware that whether you notice or not, you still use your resources, you still eat, you still interact with your budget. You are bringing your awareness back to the budget kitchen with intention and building the trust that you can and will come back.

Now, you will bring your intention to sustaining your budget kitchen, not as some static monolith but as an agile practice to meet your everchanging needs and circumstances. Where you once saw only fear, scarcity, or lack of knowledge, you begin to see the layers of existing methods and strategies. Each day, you can remember and practice that you have the power to choose and select your strategy in each new moment.

This month is about adding more depth to the simmering sauce. You have already stirred in some coziness to this budget spaghetti. Now is the time for gradually gathering materials ahead of time, for setting the table with all those people who inspire and motivate you (from your accountability buddies to your Successful Self), and for finding your own welcome and coziness each day.

After these last few months, you are uniquely qualified in the practice needed for addressing this next step of your budgetary craft, and you will continue to become even more so by inviting in more knowledge, experimentation, and growth. If your past self is like my past self, you may have imagined a future version of yourself who will be highly judgmental or disappointed. But you have cultivated compassion and gratitude for your present and past, and by doing so, you have already begun to change the habits in your future. As you practice, you can imagine that in your future, you will also be more adept at reaching for a dash of self-compassion.

Remember that you have had a couple months to practice the budget kitchen safety and ground rules. In the future, you will have even more practice with the budget kitchen safety practices than you currently do.

Cozy comfort is crafted moment by moment, day by day. You have been crafting the foundation of your present successes this whole time, and you continue to craft your future, one step at a time.

Week 9

Stocking the Staples

Although I cannot stand the smell of whisky, I have had the privilege of touring a few distilleries in Scotland, so many of which began centuries ago.

One of the things I noticed, beyond the beautiful scenery, was the particular way of discussing sustainability. While each distillery had their own brand and style, each tour alluded to the modern view of sustainability while highlighting the historical practical necessities of both avoiding waste and making profitable use of byproducts. The tours emphasized the reliance on the natural resources over the centuries to lend the distinct flavor and advantage, and the inherent ongoing obligation to preserve the natural environment to ensure the tradition could continue for centuries into the future.

You and I will not be around for centuries (still assuming you're not a vampire). But we can still weave some of this past-informed, forward-thinking, practical, efficient frugality into our budget kitchen mindset. This involves finding the habits that can be implemented consistently without complete depletion each time, while also acknowledging the reality that depletion happens. We must retain and maintain the ability to replenish.

In a budget book, you may have been expecting to find calls for frugality much sooner than this. You most likely would've expected frugality to be specifically about money, about pinching pennies. In this budget kitchen you have found you have far more resources at your disposal than mere money. It is to this broader selection of resources that you will continue to apply this concept of sustainability, renewal, and replenishment.

As you have likely observed, when your energy is depleted or waning, you are more likely to choose a money strategy that turns out to be like putting salt instead of sugar in a recipe. No wonder it can be useful to put aside the ability to make a purchase when tired or meandering towards rest. When energy is low, the actions which most replenish energy can seem like they'll take even more energy to attempt (like Green Quadrant actions of Dr. Rosier's Solve-It Grid). In times when you've settled for the less replenishing actions or left a few (or a few dozen) tasks on the back burner, it can seem like you're saving energy.

Even though it's a slower burn, these lingering tasks still drain energy.

In this way, just as with the practical frugality I saw in the distilleries, when you cultivate a constellation of healthy habits, you are more able to generate and maintain the elements you need for a healthy, financially sustainable life.

Sustainable Habits

As you have already been practicing, habits are the foundation for a functional budget kitchen. In *Atomic Habits: An Easy & Proven Way to Build Good Habits & Break Bad Ones*, James Clear shares four laws of crafting and using effective habits. Keep these Four Laws in mind this week as you continue your existing habits and layer in some savings: 1) Make it obvious, 2) Make it attractive, 3) Make it easy, 4) Make it satisfying. Even if you've read *Atomic Habits* before, it is worth considering a reread to apply these four laws in your budget kitchen.

If you have been inundated with advertisements for self-care products, you may be skeptical or wary of that last one. But one of the impactful methods Clear shares to make habits satisfying is having an accountability partner, someone you can let know of your intended habit, which can add to the satisfaction of completing the habit.

Begin to notice that this week, without judgment or expectation. Not everyone is suited to be an accountability partner in every topic, as some will judge or hold past things over you and others may be kind without inspiring you to insist on forward momentum.

What Are the Staples?

In the budget kitchen, the staples are the things you can easily preserve for a future self, whether nutrients that don't go bad, time that you don't have to spend getting the object at the grocery store each week, or the luxury of having things on hand in case you can't grocery shop for a time.

I have always assumed that the reason my grandparents kept a cabinet of earthquake food was due to growing up in San Francisco, with family or neighbors impacted in previous decades by the 1906 earthquake. On the other side of my family, my Oma and Opa grew up in the Great Depression. Needless to say, my grandparents (and parents) taught me to build and refresh an emergency or earthquake pantry, even when cash flow is tight.

As my parents and grandparents taught me, an emergency food pantry is not something stocked once and left unchecked. It can start with one extra canned good in the grocery cart. Put the one with the furthest expiration date in the emergency food pantry. Later, if you get another of the same item, you check to see if you already have one in the emergency food pantry, holding the newest ones in your emergency pantry and bringing the older one into your pantry for use. Keep it accessible, fresh, and replenished in case of an emergency, illness, or just one of those non-grocery-shopping days.

Gradually, you build up to have enough food for a day or two in an emergency, then eventually a week, always bringing the nearest expiring items to your pantry for day-to-day use.

The Extra Chai

Last week, I mentioned my Chai Challenge journey. At the time, I called it "Splurging on Student Loans" because instead of splurging on my chai or on a shopping trip, I diverted that urge to splurge towards my student loan principal balance.

When I began budget coaching, I mentioned it at times. One person accidentally took it further. Rather than choosing between the comfort item and emergency savings, they thought I'd meant to only get the comfort item after they'd put that amount in the emergency savings. When they did get the comfort item, they also paid that same amount to the emergency savings.

Needless to say, when we next gathered, I was surprised when they said that my advice had resulted in an unexpectedly large amount of emergency savings. It took a bit of puzzled listening to figure out how "my" strategy could possibly have worked so well. After we figured out how they were saving so much more than I'd expected, we had a good laugh. They were quite rightfully proud of their much more intense accomplishment.

A Flavor Note on Savings

It is important to approach the concept of emergency savings with extraordinary compassion. This is especially true for those of us at any income level who have lived or are living paycheck to paycheck and who have tried to build savings only to watch it disappear.

When money is tight and near paycheck to paycheck, it can be hard to build that emergency savings a few dollars at a time. This is especially true when you are in the situation where your cash flow has not felt like you can save ahead for large or irregular expenses. It can be really disheartening to work so hard at building up an emergency savings only to have to use it regularly.

It is tempting to ignore that emotional challenge or to believe it shouldn't be that difficult. After all, it is far easier to blame oneself, the economy, or circumstances, than to recognize that part of the recipe you're attempting is legitimately quite hard. Some of the things that feel difficult about building an emergency savings can actually be growing pains pointing to the beginning of success.

If it's taken weeks or months to build savings of $100 and there is a $99 expense, it can feel like you've practically just been dragged back to the starting line. But that's not an accurate comparison. Really, without the prep work of saving the $100, you'd be at negative $99 (and possibly soon further negative, depending on the interest rate). Can by can, cent by cent, and dollar by dollar, you'll build it back up.

When something comes up that is already hard but necessary, and it eats away at your emergency savings, go back to your kitchen ground rules: Notice, don't push the feelings away. But also, do not push away the gift your past self has given you. Your past self has made this the tiniest bit easier, which is still progress. You can build back towards a little more savings for your future Successful Self. You've now done this before.

While first beginning to save, the category can be a bit like how ultra-sensitive I am to cayenne pepper. Remember from your cooking experiments: When the sauce has way too much cayenne pepper, the sauce is not useless: someone else could eat it, it could be used incrementally to flavor a new version of the sauce, and you can use it to learn what you need for the future. If you were to just toss the sauce, despairing over the inedible quality, you might not even try for a while. Although it truly may be inedible, there are other uses, and learning is an important one.

Savings Planning Table

Figuring out the amount to save either each month or in total for a savings goal is as uniquely personal a decision as how much to have on hand for the emergency pantry, or whether cayenne pepper, garlic bread, Brussels sprouts, ice cream, or celery have any place alongside budget spaghetti.

As you consider how (and how much) to spice up your savings, you may find the following exercise useful. As with the Budget Ingredients Table, your first column may end up with different categories.

Start off with a quick Noodle Reflection (10-12 minutes). Imagine that a year in the future, you are feeling good about how your savings goals are progressing. Fill in either your monthly or total amount saved for each category one year from now. (If you have loans or do not yet have an emergency fund, several of the other categories may be $0 at this point. That's ok.) For the next column, put a number that is close to the current amount you save in a particular column, but perhaps a small amount more for the top one or two categories. In the Successful Self column, dream.

The dream can be as far in the future as you would like to imagine, and you can jot down an encouraging note from that future self to you, if you'd like.

Just as you have learned throughout this process, keeping up a steady pace of incremental changes is more sustainable than attempting a change that just doesn't fit in the current budget cookware. Instead of trying to rush to a certain dollar amount or percentage of income saved, allow yourself to think of it more like building up the staples on hand and in the emergency pantry.

The purpose this week is not to make any large changes, but rather to intentionally set up sustainable habits, to recognize those that you have built since the start of the book, and to recognize how habits work and what strategies you use. If you keep reaching for a strategy that doesn't fully meet the needs of your present and future selves for nourishment, how can you make it easier or otherwise more enticing to reach for another strategy?

Some days the nourishment is rest, some days it is a simple, basic noodle recipe with only the things on hand to save the time, energy, and money from a grocery store run when life is tough. Some days, it's a chai. Some days, it's paying down debt or adding to savings by the amount of a chai instead. Or if you're really going to take it to the extreme, you can save the chai amount first and then charge yourself another chai in savings to be able to get the chai.

No matter what, it is important to try, and your budget kitchen is a great place to practice.

Action Step

Fill in the Savings Planning Table. Start with just the Emergency Fund row. Set up a recurring transfer of at least $1 to your savings fund. The amount does not matter yet. The habit does.

What I'm Saving For	**1-Year Goal**	**Current**	**Successful Self**	**Notes**
Loan Repayment	*Monthly*			
	Total			
Emergency Fund	*Monthly*			
	Total			
Retirement / Future	*Monthly*			
	Total			
Travel / Experience	*Monthly*			
	Total			
Large Purchase / Repair	*Monthly*			
	Total			
Giving / Generosity	*Monthly*			
	Total			
Other: ___________	*Monthly*			
	Total			
TOTAL SAVINGS	*Monthly*			
	Total			

Cooking Journal

Top 3 Priorities for the week ahead

1. You are two thirds of the way through.
    i. Last month, how amazing are you for practicing and experimenting as often as you did?
    ii. What are you grateful for accomplishing the last couple months?
    iii. What are you grateful for accomplishing last week?
2. What are your Top 3 Priorities this week? Write them down.
3. Break things into subtasks if they're big. Which items are your priorities this week? Which items will be a priority for Future You?
4. What are You (of next week) grateful for accomplishing today to take good care of yourself?

Reflection Questions

1. Serving Your Whole Self

    What habits and strategies are serving you and making your life easier, either for your present moment or for tomorrow—or beyond? Where can you add more ease or energy for yourself tomorrow?
2. Gratitude for Your Host

    How do you celebrate and show gratitude for your past self when you feel the benefit of a past decision in the present moment? When there is a learning moment from a past decision, how can you show compassion, grace, and even gratitude to your past self for being on this journey, doing your best, and providing this data?

WWMSSD?

1. If you keep reaching for a strategy that doesn't fully meet the needs of your present and future selves for nourishment, how would your Successful Self make it easier or otherwise more enticing to reach for another strategy?

Week 10

Collaborate with Your Future Self

It's time for time travel!

This week, you will continue to extend your awareness to your future self, as you consider your needs and what you can do for that future self. You may already be incorporating some experimentation of how to serve your near-future self, like setting out clothes for tomorrow, prepping a lunch, or writing the top items on your to-do list. And as you gather data about what your present self needs, you can begin to get a sense of what your future self may soon or will sometimes need.

For example, if you have always loved going to the theater to see movies, even as ticket and concession prices rise, you probably expect that you would still love to do so in the future (and perhaps even as far into the future as retirement). You may decide this week that your desire to see a new movie next week is worth pressing "Save for later" on an item or two in your digital shopping cart.

By doing that, you are sharing with your future self: you are noticing that who you will be in the future has this desire or need, and that you can help take care of that today (and with the practices begun last week, your future self may even express gratitude for it!) Or perhaps you decide to prepare yourself a lovely meal at home so that you are less ravenous for highly priced snacks. That extra time and energy spent in preparation could leave you with some extra cash towards the snacks at your next movie.

This is not about cutting back on things that bring you joy and coziness. This is about increasing your coziness, taking care of yourself, in the present moment and on into the future.

Stranger Self

In *Your Future Self: How to Make Tomorrow Better Today*, Dr. Hal Hershfield illustrates how our empathy for our future self affects our care of our future self through things like retirement savings. We often hear about saving for retirement as if we are simply and logically putting aside money for ourselves, albeit in the future. But that future component can have more of an impact on our mindset than we realize. In an fMRI study, participants' brains reacted to thinking of their own future self of 10 years in the future in much the same way that their brains reacted to thoughts of a complete stranger. In further research, this impact has been found as early as 3 months from the participant's present self.

Even so, there are ways to address this, and you have already been practicing at least one of these methods. In a variety of fascinating research studies, Hershfield and colleagues have explored how letters written to and from a future self (or even a photoshopped aged-up photo of oneself) can affect present-day habits and savings choices. Our ability not only to know and perceive but also to extend empathy to our future selves can increase our present-day motivation to care for and invest in our future selves.

Even if you don't break out a quill and parchment for some time-traveling pen pal adventure, take a moment to jot down some thoughts of how you will let your future self know, "Don't be a stranger."

Cultivating Compassion and Gratitude

Whether we realize it or not, we are always in relationship with our possible selves, making or avoiding choices that affect what we are able to do and how we are able to experience our lives in future moments. From the youngest ages, we learn not only in terms of natural consequences, but also in the habits like brushing teeth, having veggies, or beginning an assignment a little earlier than the night before it is due.

Another challenge is that savings are a gift for our future self to decide what to do with. There is an inherent danger in gift-giving: once it is given, it is no longer ours to control. But just as we can choose how we give a gift to a loved one in a way that helps increase the likelihood of use for the intended purpose, so we can also make that choice when giving to our future self.

One part of building trust is to communicate. (Who knew!) We can communicate our hopes with our future self – whether in a note, journal, digital notepad or reminder system, or as a scheduled email to your future self.

Sometimes, you may worry whether your future self will honor the intention of the gift. This is a part of cultivating trust in your future self. Nobody wants to talk with someone who is grumpy when you don't do exactly what they want with their gift. It feels much nicer to say, "This may not be what you intended, but here is what I am doing and why."

As you notice gratitude for your past selves' choices to set you up for success, recognize also the ways in which you are now bearing part of the load for your past self: perhaps you were tired and could not get a task done efficiently or safely, so your past self entrusted the task to their future self. The task you do now is a gift to your past self, and recognition of your past self's needs.

As we build this trust, we craft an intentional invitation to the future selves who collaborate with our present, and we move (whether steadily or in sporadic time-jumps) towards that future Successful Self.

Temporospatial Negotiations

Let's talk about one of the most common misconceptions about saving. At first glance, it may seem like saving is a one-way deal: that you in your present moment are giving up your hard-earned cash, energy, or resources and giving that to some future self who may use it well or may squander it, and you get nothing in return.

But think of this: Have you ever made a trade with your future self?

For example, at the end of my workday, my energy reserves are often depleted, and I always have things left on my to-do list. After I allow myself some gratitude and celebration of my work for the day, I have two categories of choices: I can either trust or distrust my future self.

In practice, I might think, "I have so many other things to do tomorrow, I wouldn't decide or have time to get to this tomorrow." By doing it now even though it takes longer and more energy, I communicate my distrust of my future self (and make my future self more tired, disappointed, and groggy the next day with less sleep).

On the other hand, I might say to myself, "I will do so much better on this tomorrow after I rest, and since I have so much else to do tomorrow as well, what little steps can I take in the next 5 minutes to give as a gift to my future self to make my future self's life easier?" Sometimes this is clearing the desk, sometimes it's doing a tiny part of this or another task, sometimes it's clearing a few other little tasks so that it's easier in the morning to see what's remaining.

As you leave for the day, you may say, perhaps even aloud, "I trust my future self to take care of as much of this as possible, and to do that I need to take care of my energy now." Perhaps your future self whispers back, "Yes, take care of your energy now. I've got you."

You can increase mutual trust with your future self as you build trust in your present self, gradually extending that trust further and further into the future.

Just as you have been practicing coziness in how you arrive to be in the present moment, and extending that to your budget kitchen, let's apply these negotiation concepts to your cozy cash planning. Saving isn't just about doing things for the future self, but also trusting that future self to take care of you too, whether by taking the excess off of your plate to complete in the future or by thinking of you with compassion and understanding, knowing that you are doing your best to care for all of your obligations and needs.

With savings, you have a time machine: you can treat yourself in the future. You know you'll have a busy week next week? Treat yourself by taking care of a little something this week that'll ease your burden next week. Whether it's increasing your emergency savings, gradually paying high-interest debt (to save on all those interest payments), retirement savings, or saving for next week, take a moment now to add a little flavor for your future self.

The Noodle Frame

We want to build empathy, collaboration, and support between our present and future selves. Not only does our Successful Self know who to call for support, but all these future selves are parts of our Successful Self's story and can be helpful to collaborate with along the way. As we build our savings, we are able to give to our future; as we use what we save for either the intended purpose, an unexpected need, or another essential, we build trust and compassion for our past and future selves who hope and rely on us.

If a friend or a little one from your friends' or family's households gave you a gift from an elementary craft that they were just beginning to learn or in a style that they are just now learning about, how would you react to this gift?

Assuming that you wish to be supportive and that you want them to continue to enjoy this craft and find new ways to learn and grow, you will use your most appreciative eye to see things you truly do like, even if it is as simple as the arrangement of macaroni noodles on a picture frame.

Saving is only a part of your relationship with your future self, but it is essential in building a trusting relationship. Saving is the part where you share with your future self, where you care for your future self as you have been learning and practicing care for your present self. And your future self also shares with you and takes care of you: in the hopes and dreams, in the imagining of possible future selves when you are living your values, and in existing over a multitude of days and therefore being much more suited to taking on the bulk of burdens that are quite simply too big for a single present moment.

How lucky your future self is to have such a thoughtful friend in you, their past self. And how thoughtful and capable your future selves are in sharing the burdens you have weighing on you today.

Action Step

Reread the letter you wrote to your future self in the introduction. What have you learned and what would you write to your future self? What would your Successful Self notice about where you wanted to go and what you have accomplished so far?

Cooking Journal

Top 3 Priorities for the week ahead

1. What are you grateful for accomplishing last week?
2. What are your Top 3 Priorities this week? Write them down.
3. Break things into subtasks if they're big. Which items are your priorities this week? Which items will be a priority for Future You?
4. What are You (of next week) grateful for accomplishing today to take good care of yourself?

Reflection Questions

1. In Giving and Receiving
   How can you give another little gift today to your future self (and feel the gratitude right back

at you from the time stream there)? Continue to notice both when you are giving your future self a gift and when you are receiving a gift from your past self.

2. A Little for Tomorrow
   How will you treat your future self with a little bit of savings today?

WWMSSD?

1. Time Travel edition:What if you already are your successful future self for a past self? What advice do you already have, and what gratitude can you share for getting to where you already are? What hopes and dreams have you accomplished or set in motion further down the timestream? What's the next step forward today?

WEEK II

Your Kitchen Community

Why do we need a community?

That question has been considered, answered, and debated by historians, psychologists, theologians, neuroscientists, sociologists, philosophers, and neighbors at a barbecue. I do not know the answer. I do know that there is a yearning for connection.

So many industries thrive on selling us the concept of connection: from weddings, bars, jewelry, or gyms to social media, dating apps, and even generative AI. Sometimes, it may seem as if we are entirely dependent on one or more of these external products to achieve our need for connection—especially if a particular product is the sole method of connection for those around us. Granted, some of these products are definitely useful strategies in some situations and seasons. But in the same way that we already interact with money and our budget kitchen more than we may have thought at first, we already connect with people about money more than we may realize.

Whether with a romantic partner, kids, siblings, parents, roomies, or friends, we share our meals with others and we share our budget spaghetti with others. We figure out who are good folks to learn and cook with together, which folks we may go to when we are contemplating something that we don't truly want to desire anymore, and old friends with whom we fall cozily into old habits and patterns. Sometimes the old habits happen by muscle memory without our intention. Though cozy by way of familiarity, sometimes upon reflection, these patterns can be unpleasant, nostalgic, or somewhere in between.

This week, the goal is to begin to find and take note of the community of chefs who encourage you to keep up with the habits and practices you wish to have. It's a mutual experience, because no matter where you are in your journey, with a little kindness, you can also support your fellow budget chefs on their journey.

Accountability: Giving and Receiving

As you explore the sustainability of your habits and collaboration with your future selves, you also may have begun to notice if a present-day human is good at being an accountability buddy for a particular subject. This could just be in sending someone a little message saying, "I am planning to do this task or project..." and then at some point later saying "I did part or all of" the same or related tasks.

Your accountability buddy can help with productivity or goal attainment in a variety of circumstances. Sometimes your accountability buddy can be someone within your own household, or sometimes it's a friend or colleague.

After reading *Atomic Habits* at work, I have a colleague with whom on occasion, we will just send a random instant message about what self-care is looking like for us lately. If I want to go to the massage chairs at the gym but doubt that I will make this decision for myself by the end of the day, I will send a message to that accountability buddy saying that I'm planning to go to the gym later. If she replies with her self-care for the day or an emoji to cheer me on, then it brings it back top of mind a little later in the day; and even without a reply, I know that whenever she gets to her messages, she will see what my goal was. Sometimes just that is enough to sway my decision the way I already want it to go. Similarly, I hope when she lets me know what her self-care plans are for the day or weekend, she is able to benefit from our accountability buddy system.

While you can certainly attain goals on your own, it can be much easier to maintain and continue the habits when there is someone else who is aware of your goals. Even if working separately on similar goals, knowing that you share some hope or intent with another person can make the path seem a little clearer. By contrast, confiding in someone who perhaps has their own block regarding a certain topic can make your own roadblock seem to emerge or expand.

Just as with this entire process, you won't necessarily find the accountability buddy or methods that work perfectly for you on the first try. It takes some experimentation to see what is helpful in this moment and finding the people who are able not to be (or need you to be) a therapist or personal coach, but simply a moment of presence towards your individual goals.

As you go about your week and reflect on your journey so far, when have you successfully noticed nonjudgmentally when there are people whose money practices are theirs and not yours to affect, hold onto, or take responsibility for?

We are not here to fix each other. Just like when you came to this budget kitchen, it was not that you were broken and needed fixing, but that you had skills that you needed to discover, recognize, and practice for yourself.

At the Table

Over meals or snacks, we talk about our hopes, dreams, and what's important to us.

We may talk about a hope for the future, whether childhood goals, retirement, visiting a place or person, a vision of our community, and lifelong dreams. We may say we've tried or read of something new, and a fellow experimenting chef might be intrigued, give themselves permission to be creative as well, or have another thought that percolates on the back burner of their mind for us to try another time.

The reality of being in community means that you also may have a wacky relative or coworker who suggests some odd social media trend that seems too good to be true or maybe doesn't seem healthy at all (perhaps like time travel spaghetti? That person is definitely a nerd!) So, with some healthy skepticism, you do a bit of your own research and check in later with a doctor (someone with actual credentials for comprehensive holistic planning for the stage you're working on).

In *The Light We Carry: Overcoming in Uncertain Times*, Michelle Obama describes the importance of her practice of gathering, assembling, and maintaining relationships with her "kitchen table" friends and mentors. Those at our "kitchen table" are the people who support us and who we support, and with whom we may safely be honest and fully present. Who are the people with whom you are able to more objectively see your strengths, aspirations, and struggles—empowering and encouraging you to find the next steps?

In cultivating these core supportive relationships, just as in all other elements of the budget kitchen, keep arriving and keep up with your kitchen safety ground rules. I sometimes avoid replying to a text after a certain amount of time because I feel like it's been too long, but often, my dearest friends are just grateful to connect, perhaps also feeling that they also wished to reach out sooner. Times and seasons change: sometimes we are busier, and sometimes others are busier. Small moments of connection regularly, whether given or received, can help sustain us and our friendships.

A brief note on supportive energy:

Sometimes we need more supportive energy, and sometimes we provide more supportive energy. This is not the same as being dependent on someone or having someone dependent on you. While this inevitably happens in certain stages of life, parenthood, community, or illness, being able to ask for help is not the same as being dependent on someone, and being able to provide support to someone is not the same as being a sole or primary caregiver.

While you may have or be dependent on someone else at various times in your life, that is not what this concept of a supportive community is about. In this community, everyone is capable of learning, growth, taking care of our needs to the best of our abilities, and finding or being pointed towards resources that we can use for our goals. In supportive community, this is all achieved without paternalism, dependence, condescension, or control.

Seasonal Community

Not everyone needs to be in your budget kitchen all the time. Just like with certain family members who may come only for the holidays, some people have such exacting standards or expectations that it is better for everyone's sanity if they are out of the kitchen. Sometimes in a group setting, another family member or two can chat and distract either you or the more particular guest, or comfort and help out. Sometimes, it's just you, and you breathe, move the dishes forward, and remember you can only do what you can do. And that's what you're doing.

The budget kitchen can be like that too, and even more annoyingly, sometimes you get talking heads jumping in from the news or social media, with opinions and perspectives about budget decisions from society at large. These ideas and opinions may come from people who will never even know you or your budget kitchen. Personally, I can't stand avocados, so I remain immune by default to any discussions of avocado toast, but people with these sorts of criticisms seem like they're always popping up.

You may also realize that some of your current friends are not the ideal folks with whom to discuss your budget kitchen experimentation, especially if you are discovering different spending in this season. That's ok. Sometimes you can form other points of connection with them, or sometimes you will find that fewer points of connection will work better in this season.

In the second week of *The Artist's Way: A Spiritual Path to Higher Creativity*, Julia Cameron writes: "Do not expect your blocked friends to applaud your recovery. That's like expecting your best friends at the bar to celebrate your sobriety. How can they when their own drinking is something they want to hold onto?" If your creativity in the budget kitchen has been blocked or impeded by unintentional habits, others who shared in those patterns may not be as joyful as you are when you begin to unblock and explore. On the other hand, you may be surprised to find some folks who are delighted, some who want to join in, and some who are more tentative with more of a wait-and-see-if-this-sticks stance. It is important to be aware of where your external support lies, while maintaining your core internal support as well.

Building Support that Lasts

When I was studying for the CFP exam, I would often let my fellow grad school classmates know that I'd be on a particular video-call link while I studied. That time rarely worked for them, but the possibility that one might show up was oddly helpful for my focus during those times.

In the ADHD community, we call this idea "body doubling," the phenomenon of a task being easier to complete when someone else is nearby (or potentially nearby), even if doing something else.

Whether you find yourself connecting with your "kitchen table" friends and mentors, joining an ADHDer body doubling video call, or finding that friend or colleague with whom you can remember to breathe when the budget kitchen starts feeling crowded, the goal this week is to invite and build a support network with intention and discernment.

Not everyone who shows up needs to get invited in. Not everyone who is helpful for a time is helpful all the time or for all circumstances. We all need accountability, support, and community in the present. And your Successful Self is grateful when you call in this support.

Action Step

Identify one person to be your budget kitchen accountability partner, someone who will ask how it is going without judgment. Talk with them this week about it and ask if they are willing. Then set a recurring 15-minute check-in, such as meeting up for tea, a text exchange, or a call.

Cooking Journal

Top 3 Priorities for the week ahead

1. What are you grateful for accomplishing last week?
2. What are your Top 3 Priorities this week? Write them down.
3. Break things into subtasks if they're big. Which items are your priorities this week? Which items will be a priority for Future You?
4. What are You (of next week) grateful for accomplishing today to take good care of yourself?

Reflection Questions

1. When It's Not Mine to Hold
   As you go about your week, and reflect on your journey so far, when have you successfully noticed nonjudgmentally when there are people whose money practices are theirs and not yours to affect, hold onto, or take responsibility for?

2. Amplifying Success
   Who are the people with whom you are able to more objectively see your strengths, aspirations, and struggles? Who are the people empowering and encouraging you to find the next steps?

WWMSSD?

1. This week and going forward, you will practice finding the accountability buddies, fellow budget chefs, and your kitchen table friends and mentors. Imagine that your Successful Self has you on speed dial and is always ready to send a little gratitude your way as you connect with your budget chef community. Write down what your Successful Self would say, and either put it somewhere you can easily see it or start a little collection jar to watch these notes multiply over time.

WEEK 12

Welcome Home

Welcome!

As you arrive at this chapter, how bizarre is it to think that you are now the future self of when you began this book?

You have done so much for your present self along the way, acknowledging the skills and experience sourced from your past self. In the last weeks, as you extend that care to your future self through preparation, savings, and sustainable energy replenishment, perhaps you also allowed your future self to take care of something for you. Time travel can be a bit tricky, but hopefully, you are beginning to build some mutual trust and companionship.

Each day when you arrive, set up, prepare, and share, you are building a collaborative relationship to research and explore the best, most energy-efficient, and coziest ways to create that comfy feeling of home for yourself. Even if you cannot know exactly how your future self will show up, you know that your future self is steadily on the way to you.

And so, as you arrive at this final week of the book, breathe a sigh of welcome to you, future self of the one who began this book, and to your future selves yet to come.

This is your budget kitchen, and you are preparing an ever-cozier place from which to grow.

The Winding Path

Over the years, I have had not just clients, but friends, family members, and acquaintances tell me that because of how I talked openly and freely about money, they began their first budget, began to save, or experienced some financial levity or freedom. As the Tenth Doctor said in the *Doctor Who* episode, Blink: "People assume that time is a strict progression of cause to effect, but actually from a non-linear, non-subjective viewpoint, it's more like a big ball of wibbly wobbly time-y wimey stuff." This path you are on can feel anything but straightforward once the noodles start cooking.

Return for a moment to the priorities and goals you set at the beginning of these 12 weeks. How distant this might have felt, how uncertain about what could even be possible. You cannot know what the future will hold or know for sure what the destination will be. You can, however, pick a direction that meets your needs, goals, and values in the present, and you can set yourself up for success in keeping that ability open for the future as well.

As mentioned in the discussion of emergency savings, a little more savings here or there can be a difficult new practice. And when an emergency comes up, the practice can take on a harsh emotional flavor if the savings tally resets towards zero. But having any emergency savings can help decrease the possible debt an emergency may have necessitated and therefore also the drag of interest on the next steps forward.

Alternatively, you will find at times that having some staples in the emergency pantry allows you to address your needs and values differently. For example, someone I knew began saving a small amount from each paycheck of a very small income. When a family member was affected by a natural disaster, the savings enabled them to send some money in support. For a time, the savings was gone, but that also had been the purpose: to enable greater choices in times when just the amount of the paycheck was not up to the task.

I have found that there is a greater benefit in conversations than merely to those involved in the conversation, as each person may then share their winding path with others along the way. It is inspiring to see a dream draw a friend forward and to watch the accumulation of their joyful efforts. Similarly, our presence on the path may be of greater benefit to others than we realize. The more we are able to chat and listen compassionately about money, saving, thinking ahead or more in the moment, the more we and others around us can have a safe space to think about what we want, need, and value. Even just being able to talk freely about it in a genuinely safe "budget kitchen" space can help make a difference in unexpectedly beautiful ways.

Setting the Table for Your Future Self

This journey has been about building confidence in the things that are actually in your present and future self's control. Be sure to acknowledge that, while there are always things you can't control, you can still do your best given the circumstances to provide care for your present and future selves. Each time you do so, you are nurturing a growing confidence in your own capability while maintaining awareness of the real boundaries of the cooking area at this time.

Continue to pay attention to how you are dealing with your future self. Notice if you and your future self are being reasonable, collaborative, and kind with each other. Keep your awareness sensitive enough to notice some of those times when your future self is trying to tap your present self on the shoulder and say, "Hey, I don't know if you can hear me, but you might just want to consider a different path here." Even if you really don't want to follow your future self's advice in the moment, consider how to set the table in a way that could allow for that future self to also get what they want. What slight adjustment could you make to leave room for your future self to show up to the table?

Your selves of present, past, and future all have useful data and ideas for you to explore. Some of those ideas will seem like useful things to start on in the present, while others will seem better suited for a future self to explore. In those cases, you can imagine your future self adjusting some safety goggles and saying, "Ok, I've got this." If your future self is feeling silly or it's Halloween, your future self will throw in a gleeful, maniacal "Muahaha." Well said, future self! For science! (Distant evil laughter...)

As you keep the playful experimentation, try new recipes or ways to spice it up little by little, make notes of the results, bringing in gratitude for the new knowledge you're gaining. Hold onto what works and let go of what is no longer your style or what doesn't work for this season, with gratitude for its place in your life.

Just as a close friend may at times forget or need a little reminder, we can set up the habits and systems to ease the burden on our future self as well. For a fun nerdy example of how to create a little room at the table for our future self without having to make much of a change now, check out Thaler and Benartzi's Save More Tomorrow research and how radically useful it can be to set automatic increases of savings rates that coincide with anticipated raises. Basically, if you want to slightly increase your retirement savings and can set it up to do so when you get a pay increase, then you can still enjoy the slight pay increase from the raise while knowing you're also saving more.

On Being a Host

Imagine that you are preparing for your future self's arrival as if you are their host for an extended holiday. As with any hosting experience, there are three main questions to be able to welcome in your future self.

First, how can you help your future self feel welcome and cared for upon arrival? When you notice your future self will have a preference that doesn't perfectly align with what you want to do in the moment, pause and breathe. This is a natural tradeoff situation, and you are capable of navigating multiple underlying needs and balancing your present and future with intention. Can you make a slight adjustment to the strategy to make it easier for your future self to show up to the table?

Second, how do you set your future selves up for success, both with data-informed expectations and by preparing a little more ahead of time, when possible?

And third, how do you build trust in your future selves? Your future self doesn't have to be that terrifying guest who judges you for every little speck of dust. Your future self may jump in and say "oh gosh, you have had a really rough time of it, let me take care of the dishes for you."

One flavorful and complex dish you can prepare for your future self is a Long-Term Financial Goal (LTFG). You can define long-term however you'd like, but be sure to put it far enough into the future that it feels attainable. Jot down what you are doing or will do to make it attainable within that timeframe, starting with a step or a habit to practice in the next 48 hours.

Ever On and On

In each moment, you are receiving attempts at support (whether intentional or inadvertent) from the efforts of your past self. Express gratitude: this is a part of your success story. As a society, we tend to glorify the ultimate successes and innovations, only celebrating a long series of experiments when the ending of the success story is already known.

But that is not what this budget kitchen is about. Your big successes here are in the everyday experiments and moments of growth and gratitude. You are living your success story, even though you don't know yet what your future self will end up seeing as the plotline of the success.

The evidence you have gathered is clear: you are capable of making decisions.

Even when you reflect or find that those decisions are not in your best interest or that the strategies do not meet the needs you'd hoped they would, you have still made the little decisions that lead to that particular aftertaste. And you are beginning to know and recognize these moments as the additional (if unintentional) culinary experiments that they are. You record the data and results in your Cooking Journal. You may even have found that even if you don't find a pattern right now, it emerges later.

You don't need to have all the answers today, and there will never be a time when you have all the answers. Therefore, it is safe and practical to keep coming back to these little experiments and moments in which you can learn and grow.

Though these 12 weeks are coming to a close, your Successful Self sees this as an origin story prequel. In the months ahead, continue noticing the ways in which your past self has given you the gifts of important preparation and lessons which support or inform your present and future selves.

Hold space for compassion and keep giving little gifts to your future self. Express gratitude. Rest: your future self needs to be rested just as you also need rest. Truly replenishing rest today can be a mutually beneficial collaboration between you and your future self. Check in on your Top 3 Priorities regularly. Let yourself noodle over it when you realize there may be a little bit of savings or prep work that you know your future self will appreciate not having to think about. When in doubt, do the next tiny step or experiment.

Ultimately, your long-term financial goal is not a destination but a direction. Like a compass, your budgeting will not always point the same direction from you. Instead, it is just another tool to navigate your path.

Like a cooked spaghetti noodle, the path will not stay straight, rigid, and unbending. Instead, the path will curve, meander, and maybe get a bit messy and fun, just like spaghetti. That is life. You have proven that you can grow through mess and into comfort and coziness.

Welcome home.

Action Step

Name one long-term financial goal. Write down what needs to be true in 6 months or a year to be on track. Then write down one thing you will do this week toward it. Put it on your calendar, your fridge, your phone lock screen, your bathroom mirror.

Cooking Journal

Top 3 Priorities for the week ahead

1. What are you grateful for accomplishing last week?
2. What are your Top 3 Priorities this week? Write them down.
3. Break things into subtasks if they're big. Which items are your priorities this week? Which items will be a priority for Future You?
4. What are You (of next week) grateful for accomplishing today to take good care of yourself?

Reflection Questions

1. Long-Term Financial Goal (LTFG)
   What is one long-term financial goal that would genuinely change your life? What would need to be true in 6 months for you to be on track toward that goal?

2. Setting the Table
   How can you help your future self (near or far) feel welcome and cared for? How do you set your future selves up for success, whether through data-informed expectations or by preparing ahead of time? How do you build trust in your future self today by honoring the commitments of your past self?

WWMSSD?

1. Think of a time you made financial progress and then experienced a setback. What did you do next?
2. How does your Successful Self handle unexpected financial setbacks?

Conclusion

Keeping It Cozy

I am not a chef.

I don't always enjoy or have the energy to cook. For me, meal planning involves mentally calculating the absolute minimum number of times I can manage to cook and still have enough food and variety to eat for the week. This is how I used to feel about budgeting, so I live in hope for a future self to be a little happier with cooking.

Over years of "adulting," I have found recipes that nourish well enough without taking too much time or energy, and recipes that fill the home with a cozy aroma that just seeps into my bones like crawling under a fluffy blanket after a long workday.

In some seasons, that recipe is spaghetti (or some other pasta, depending on how much energy I have to operate a fork or clean up the sauce splatter after our meal).

Spaghetti was one of my grandma's preferred recipes. In so many of my childhood memories, she wore an old floral shirt, her "spaghetti shirt" while cooking spaghetti. She always said that if she didn't wear that shirt, she inevitably found herself wearing a white shirt that showed every speck of sauce. She would modify the recipe based on the preferences of those joining for the meal and bring frozen containers of sauce with us on vacations.

Although she didn't think she was good at math, numbers, or budgeting, my grandma had all the practice to craft a cozy budget right there in that cozy spaghetti. She arrived intentionally for the task at hand. She used the recipe as a strategic starting point, drawing on the wisdom from prior generations and yet tailored to the present moment. She prepared resources in advance for her future self and loved ones, so that we could all have a cozy vacation together.

My grandparents showed me that the life and values we aspire to for ourselves or our loved ones is not something that is shown merely by some large event or celebration. It is in every moment we choose to live or prepare to live those values. It is in the cleanup, the fluffing of pillows, taking in friends who needed a place to stay or supporting their journey towards self-sufficiency. It's in the checkout lanes at the grocery store, in large festive gatherings, or just a few of us sitting quietly together on the porch, sipping from steaming mugs as the sun rises.

I often told them that if I could live a life even 10% as loving as they were, I would be one of the most amazingly compassionate people. In truth, I'm glad when I attain even 1%. Like interest on a savings account, it may not be much, but it sure feels good to grow with purpose.

Like my grandma's spaghetti recipe, a budget is never finished. Life changes, income changes, values evolve. You grow, connect, learn, and thrive. You bring nourishment for yourself and all those you care for. You bring in your breath and awareness. You know you are always coming back to your budget kitchen and the cozy recipes you craft here.

And here at the end of this book, take a comfortable seat in your budget kitchen. Hold that warm mug of tea and enjoy the view from the window. Smile along with that glimmer of your Successful Self, knowing that even as you complete this book, each moment is a new beginning.

Action Step

Write your Top 5 wins. Tell one person. Set one New Month Resolution. And come back to your Budget Kitchen whenever you need it. It will always be here.

Cooking Journal: Next Steps

Top 3 Priorities for the week ahead

1. What are you grateful for accomplishing these last 12 weeks?
2. What are your Top 3 Priorities for the next month? Write them down.
3. What are your Top 3 Priorities for the next week? Write them down. Notice the overlap, and how you're preparing for the month as you plan the week.
4. What are You (of next week) grateful for accomplishing today to take good care of yourself?

Reflection Questions

1. What are your Top 5 wins from working through this book?
2. How has your relationship with money changed (even a little) since Week 1?
3. What is your New Month Resolution for next month?
4. Who will you share this book with?

WWMSSD?

1. Come back to your Successful Self description from Week 1. What would you add or change now?

Next steps:

1. Return Again
   Pencil in a reminder (or reminder notification) in your calendar to pick this book up again,

whether a few months from now, a birthday, at the New Year, or some other time.

2. Gather with Gratitude
   Schedule a group reading with your Kitchen Community in 3-6 months (give a few of them some time to get through their first time through if they want to go solo at first)
3. Remember seasons
   Keep refreshing and learning new things.

EMERGENCY RESOURCES

www.budgetspaghetti.com/resources

ACKNOWLEDGEMENTS

Writing this book is a continuation of earlier work and even earlier lessons in life, all of which cascade exponentially into ever more abundant opportunities for gratitude. I thank as many of you along the way as I think of, and will continue to do so.

To attempt to acknowledge all those whose work, research, companionship, or lives have had an impact on this project feels both impossible and overwhelming. I thought writing the book would be the hard part. Trying to define and contain my gratitude within a static page seems the more impossible task, but I will give it a go.

To the teams at Tremendous Leadership and at Live Oak Studio in Berkeley, for guiding me through the process of bringing this dream into reality.

To Dr. Chia-Li Chien, for your support and encouragement throughout my financial planning education. When you were introducing me, a year early, as a successful soon-to-be published author, you helped silence my inner critic so that I could hear my own truth. And to all of my professors, teachers, and academic role models throughout the years.

To The Naming Project and to my Mills people for helping me find my voice. Thank you especially Cass and Jenny, for all of the discussions and insights during this writing project and throughout the years.

To Sydney Woodward, for getting me into pro bono planning, and to the pro bono committee and board of the Financial Planning Association of San Francisco. For decades, I used to have a different favorite day of the year; now, it's Financial Planning Day. Incredible.

My amazing book clubs, bookstores, and libraries, with particular gratitude to my *Artist's Way* digital cohort—your accountability kept me coming back to the Morning Pages from which this book emerged.

To the teams of The Hero's Journal, Passion Planner, and ADHD Center of West Michigan: you made it possible to focus on making my dream a reality. There are innumerable individuals who have inspired me throughout my life as I dreamed of becoming an author, a budget coach, and a financial planner. You know who you are, thank you.

To my family, especially Josh and kiddos, my constant teachers in love and community. I love you. Josh, thank you for all your support even as I woke you hours early when I left to write each morning, and for all the line editing. Thank you, Dad, for all the conversations over the years, starting long before that 2nd grade budgeting experience.

To all my early readers along the way, especially: Kara Bestler, Katherine Burke, Tiara Byerly, Jessica Daley, Bailey Davis, and Masami Kiyono. You may barely recognize the phrasing all these iterations later, but I thank you all for consistently calling me back to the heart of the message.

And to you, amazing reader! I hope your cozy budget nourishes and sustains your dreams. Thank you for reading!

ABOUT THE AUTHOR

Anne Serrano, CFP® is a nerd and financial planner. With a B.A. in Economics and Ethnic Studies and an M.S. in Financial Planning, Anne also has over a decade of experience helping people with their budgets. She believes that with honesty, self-compassion, and a healthy helping of coziness, you can design your budget to support the life (and cat) you love.

www.anneserrano.com

www.ingramcontent.com/pod-product-compliance
Lightning Source LLC
Chambersburg PA
CBHW050527240926
51846CB00003B/726
* 9 7 8 1 9 6 1 2 0 2 9 0 0 *